A Reference Architecture

for

Enterprise Architecture

According to EA^3

Documented in EA^3

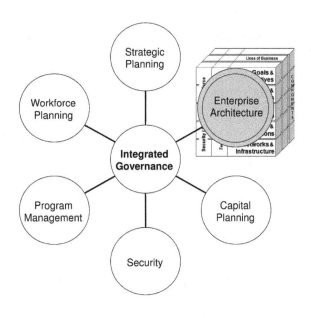

First Edition
Phil Woodworth

Dedications

To my wife, Jane, and two children Thomas and Charlotte, for their love and patience during the production of the book while I swung between procrastination and slavish devotion to its completion, and everything in between.

Acknowledgements

To Dr Scott Bernard, for going public with his ideas, experiences and insights into Enterprise Architecture (EA), and in the process lifting the discipline of EA.

To the students of the EA certification training programs I delivered who asked the big hard questions that prevented me from resting on my laurels and forced me to understand better and deeper the concepts within Dr Bernard's approach, and in the various other EA approaches that it builds on and refers to.

To Scott McBride and John Jessup, for their tuition and generosity of knowledge during my own induction into Dr Bernard's approach to Enterprise Architecture.

And finally, to my peer reviewers, Richard Jenkins and James Watson, who gave up their valuable time to review the book and to share their own knowledge and experiences on EA.

Copyediting by Jera Editing Services.

Preface

While there are a number of Enterprise Architecture (EA) frameworks available, and a lot of good books to guide organisations on what they should do and what EA should deliver, organisations and individuals lack a target architecture for their EA function, leaving many decisions to be made in the absence of sound, communicable and transparent views as to why and what they are striving for when doing EA.

This book endeavours to further lift the discipline of EA by filling this gap and providing a reference architecture for an EA function. Providing an outline of the key drivers and components of the EA function, including the influences on, and objectives of, EA, and the business and technology processes and resources used to perform EA to address these drivers.

After all, an EA function is just like any other functional area of activity within an organisation, and like any other functional area has its own set of goals and initiatives, customers and suppliers, people and activities, and data and technology. That is, its changeable components. Given that the purpose of EA is to help understand the key changeable components of any area of common goal and activity, then an EA function's changeable components can be documented in their current and future state in the same way EA espouses that, to facilitate planning and implementation, it should be done for other functional areas or 'enterprises'.

A reference architecture approach has been used because it is a proven method of assisting the scoping and definition of a domain of interest. One that works on the assumption that while all enterprises are subject to their own set of influences and priorities, enterprises within a given industry or discipline that base their operating models on proven best practices and positive real world experiences will arrive at a similar future state, albeit with slight differences. Enterprises, however, rarely have the perfect knowledge of best practices, access to the right level of knowledge and skills or time to achieve this natural future state. So to help organisations reach this optimal state quicker and with fewer mistakes and false starts, reference architectures are made available providing a proven and communicable target. The Telecommunications industry framework and the financial industry's Information FrameWork (IFW) are examples of reference architectures available to enterprises in these industries. These frameworks provide the foundations on which these enterprises can base their planning, communications and implementations, with a higher degree of confidence and certainty that they are paying attention to the right things.

To ensure the reference architecture incorporates the best practices, skills and experiences for Enterprise Architecture, the architecture is based on the concepts and principles of EA outlined in Dr Scott Bernard's book, 'An Introduction to Enterprise Architecture, EA[3]', and his EA training program and certification course material[1], which have both contributed to building on the EA experiences and practices of EA practitioners over the past two decades.

Also, to illustrate and support understanding of the concepts and principles covered in the book and training program the reference architecture has been documented according to the example EA[3] framework and artefacts discussed in the book and training course referenced above. In this way, they serve as an example of a real and relevant architecture; one that contains analysis, artefacts, linkages and management views of an EA function's changeable components, and that addresses an oft-cited criticism of EA that there is a lack of good and realistic examples of enterprise architecture.

A core element of the EA[3] approach is the use of tools and a repository. EA tools are often referred to as a distraction, 'time waster' and unnecessary, and the value of using an EA tool over standard office products questioned. To help demonstrate the potential and the right and successful use of a tool in support of EA, all model diagrams, component documentation and relationships, tables and lists have been generated and documented using IBM's Enterprise Architecture tool, System Architect.

---

[1] Formerly the Carnegie Mellon University (CMU) EA accreditation training program.

Intended Audience

A Reference Architecture for Enterprise Architecture - According to EA³, Documented in EA³ targets a few specific audience groups.

First, the book is intended to provide additional information that readers of Dr Scott Bernard's book, and students of his and other EA courses, can use to further aid their learning and understanding of EA concepts and the EA³ approach to EA.

Second, as a reference architecture of an EA function, the book intends to provide the details of the components that need to be planned for, described and implemented to deliver an EA capability, and how to align these to the needs of the organisation. The book in this respect is applicable to the work of EA sponsors EA stakeholders, EA managers, Chief Architects, and Enterprise Architects.

As an example target architecture and transition plan, the book explains and demonstrates how and what it means to improve the delivery of services by taking an EA approach to business and IT process and resource planning and oversight. The book in this respect is applicable to the work of executives, business managers, business planners, business analysts, and IT architects, managers and technical staff.

Organisation of the Book

The book is divided into 9 sections, one for each layer within the EA³ framework, one for each of the framework's common threads and a final section containing various potential EA program and transition plans depending on the drivers and goals of the EA function.

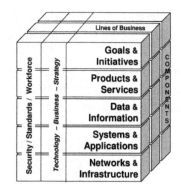

Layers

The layers document the key components within the target EA function. Their definitions, linkages, reason for being and relevance to the EA function are discussed and explained. These sections are to help explain the why, what and how of EA, specifically:

Section 1 - The EA Goals and Initiatives Layer - This section outlines the common influences, drivers, stakeholders and customers of an EA function, and the set of objectives and performance measures the EA function should target to address these. In doing so, it aims to demonstrate how and what to gather and document about the current and future strategic and tactical drivers of any enterprise.

Section 2 - The EA Products and Services Layer - This section documents the key services and activities that an EA function needs to perform to meet the objectives and performance measures set for the function. Clear links between the services and activities and targeted objectives are provided in order to support the implementation planning of the services and activities. In providing this detail, this section aims to demonstrate the documentation of the future state the business products and services must achieve to address the strategic and tactical drivers.

Section 3 - The EA Data and Information Layer - This section documents the information flows required to support, and that are produced by, the services and activities of an EA function, and the structure and rules of the data involved in these exchanges. In doing so, it demonstrates how to model the future data and information requirements of an enterprise.

Section 4 - The EA Systems and Applications Layer - This section illustrates the IT systems required to support the recommended or required automation solutions for the information flows and services of the EA function. In doing so, it demonstrates how to derive and model the future systems and application requirements of any enterprise.

Section 5 - The EA Networks and Infrastructure Layer - This section highlights any networks or infrastructure considerations relevant to the IT systems solutions identified in the EA systems and applications layer.

Threads

The threads highlight the common considerations that must be given to all components across all layers. For example, when planning, doing and enabling EA, what are the organisational and workforce considerations, the business and technology standards that are relevant, that already exist or must be taken into account when planning or overseeing change, and what are the relevant security requirements? Specifically:

Section 6 - 8 - The Common Threads - These sections outline the security, standards and workforce-related plans and considerations for the EA function.

EA Program/Transition Plan

Section 9 - The EA Program/Transition Plan - This section outlines different capabilities an EA function may implement depending on the needs of the enterprise implementing the EA function. It demonstrates how to use strategy and business component priorities and linkages down through the layers to help plan and formulate the investments needed to transform and execute the EA.

To aid decision-making within the enterprise through the provision of right and accurate information about core current enterprise components and their linkages, and to target changeable components, the layer and thread sections are documented in a question-oriented fashion.

At the end of each section are a number of tips and suggestions on how to assess and identify what is important to the timing of architecting the layer or thread for the enterprise or EA function.

How to Use the Book

As an Aid to Learning and Performing EA

If using the book as an aid to EA learning, one should read the book sequentially, starting with the layers and threads to gain a good appreciation of the concepts behind EA and how it aims to improve planning and oversight decision-making from a strategic, business and technology perspective.

While the subject detail of the diagrams, catalogues, matrices and EA management views are mostly irrelevant to any enterprise other than an EA function, and therefore can be glanced over, the diagrams, catalogues, matrices and EA management views provide realistic examples of the EA component documentation and assessment that should be, and typically are, documented and analysed when doing EA.

Reading through the layers will also help to understand how each layer drives or influences the architecture of the next, and how the core components and their interrelationships are critical to deriving the right change in lower layers. This is a fundamental concept of EA that helps to achieve the right degree of alignment between strategy, business and technology planning.

In the 'What should be considered when documenting and analysing the...' sub-sections at the end of each layer, a number of business and technology related topics that are typically encountered by and need to be addressed or considered within an EA function are discussed, providing background information, insights and guidelines to aid in the decision-making processes associated with doing EA.

As an Aid to Planning and Implementing an EA Function

If using the book to help define the scope and intent of an EA Function or to plan and manage the implementation of an EA function, in addition to understanding the material within the book the following is also recommended:

- Reference the content directly to help build the case and rationale for an EA function as the material applies the same EA principles and approach to the EA function as to a broader enterprise. Thus helping to explain and justify how EA and the EA function will deliver value to its enterprise, as well as providing material to support the organisation to make the types of decisions necessary when performing EA and developing an EA capability.

- Follow the guidelines in the 'For the EA function' sub-section of the 'What should be considered when documenting and analysing the ... layer' sections at the end of each layer chapter to help:
    o Assess your EA function's current capabilities
    o Document its future requirements
    o Leverage the content and principles within the reference architecture.
- Finally, read through the EA Program Plan/Transition Plan section to identify the strategic EA capability(s) applicable to your organisation's definition and intent for EA. This will allow relevant components within the Layers and Thread sections to be targeted and prioritised.

Table of Contents

Table of Figures

Table of Tables

Table of Tables

Introduction

This section summarises the key concepts and principles of Dr Scott Bernard's approach to Enterprise Architecture (EA). It is not intended to be a detailed explanation of the concepts; for this, refer to Dr Bernard's book directly or attend his certification training program. It is however meant to provide an introduction to the concepts and principles of his approach that the reference architecture is based on.

- EA is one of a number of functional areas that contributes to an integrated approach to managing business and information technology (IT) processes and resources.
- An enterprise is an area of common activity and goals, either within an organisation, of an organisation, or across several organisations, where information and other resources are exchanged.
- Changes to an enterprise are driven from 3 levels:

    1. Strategic directions and goals from the executive level
    2. Business priorities and performance requirements from the business or management level
    3. Information technology issues and opportunities from the ICT function or technical level.

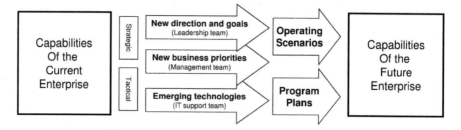

Figure 1: EA drivers and approach concepts of operations

- EA outcomes help to:
    - Achieve strategic goals that depend on IT resources
    - Improve business performance by maximising IT efficiency
    - Support the desire of executives and managers to have strategic priorities/business requirements drive IT solutions

- o Link multiple IT networks, systems, applications, services, and databases across the entire enterprise
- o Share information between lines of business
- o Integrate several forms of applications and local/wide area networks that lack open standards
- o Reduce duplicative IT resources across the enterprise
- o Protect data and IT assets that rely on enterprise-wide approaches
- o Maximise the effective use of limited budgets
- o Improve human capital management in IT knowledge/skill areas.
- The value propositions for EA are:
  - o Strategic Alignment - alignment, agility and performance
  - o Business Performance - right processes, done right
  - o Technology Solutions - solutions meet business requirements and address business priorities
  - o Technology Cost Control - IT becomes less complex, more efficient and standardised.
- EA is both a management program and a documentation process:
  - o As a management program EA provides a strategic, integrated approach to IT resource planning. An EA program is part of an overall governance process that
    - Determines resource alignment - uses architecture to identify and assess that processes and resources are the right investments from a strategic and performance perspective
    - Develops standardised policy - takes an enterprise-wide approach to determining the right standards
    - Enhances decision support - brings accurate and complete information and analysis of the enterprise to planning and oversight meetings
    - Oversees resource development activities - reviews solution plans and designs for compliance and fit with standards and future directions, i.e. things are done right.
  - o As a documentation method, EA provides:
    - An EA Approach - a modelling framework and implementation methodology to ensure the repeatability and standardisation of architecture efforts
    - Current Architecture - views of as-is strategies, processes and resources key for gap analysis, duplication analysis, etc.
    - Future Architecture - views of to-be strategies, processes and resources against which future investments are communicated and reviewed for compliance
    - An EA Management Plan - to summarise the decisions made about the current strategies, process and resources and the resultant portfolio of work and future strategies, processes and resources based on those decisions.

- EA's distinguishing features are:
    - Enterprise-wide views - taking an enterprise-wide perspective to application of standards, identification of reuse and duplication removal
    - Strategy and business drives technology solutions - IT investments are evaluated in light of their support for priority strategies and performance issues
    - Helps improve the performance of large, complex enterprises - it's an approach aimed at helping organisations manage the complexity associated with large scale operations.
- EA requires the following 6 core elements to be established to provide a complete approach:

    1. Integrated governance - identifies the planning, decision-making, and oversight processes and groups that will determine how the enterprise architecture needs to be developed and maintained as part of the organisation's overall governance.

    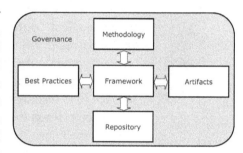

    Figure 2: EA Core Elements

    2. An EA methodology - specific steps to establish and maintain an EA program, via the selected approach.

    3. An EA framework - the scope of the overall architecture and the type and relationship of the various sub-architecture levels and threads. Not all frameworks allow for segments, or integrate strategy, business and technology.

    4. EA artefacts - the types and methods of documentation to be used in each sub-architecture area, including strategic analyses, business plans, internal controls, security controls, and models of workflow, databases, systems, and networks.

    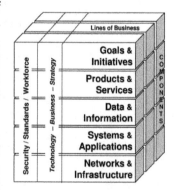

    5. EA tools and repository - the EA website, documentation database, and the software applications (tools) that are used for modelling, analysis, and reporting. The repository's design should reflect the underlying architecture approach.

    Figure 3: EA³ Framework

6. EA best practices - proven ways to plan, document or implement parts of the overall architecture or sub-architecture.

- The EA methodology is a four-phased approach divided into 20 steps. The phases and steps are principally sequential, with each phase/step building on and using the outputs from the previous phase or step. Phases and/or steps should iterate on a regular basis adding onto the content, detail, etc. of its outputs each time. This will allow subsequent phases and/or steps to in turn work on new and additional inputs in turn.

  Phase 1 - EA Establishment. Contains steps for establishing sponsorship, key roles, key governance integrations and communications plan.

  Phase 2 - EA Framework and Tool Selection. Contains steps for selecting and establishing the framework and tools required to support the documentation and use of the EA

  Phase 3 - Documenting the EA. Contains steps for documenting and assessing the current state, and planning the future architecture and EA management plan.

  Phase 4 - Using the EA. Contains steps for the using the results of the documentation and assessment to work with other governance functions and refreshing the documentation and assessments.

- Other forms of architectures are either best practices or sub-architectures of EA. Enterprise Architecture uses other forms of architecture to help document, assess, plan and oversee layers of the architecture. Examples of sub-architecture include:
  - Information architecture
  - Information engineering
  - Business activity modelling
  - Data architecture
  - Service-oriented architecture.

Section 1 – The Goals and Initiatives of the EA function

EA is one of the principal methods of optimising business and IT alignment. Specifically, it tries to ensure that the IT department's focus and spend supports and addresses future directions, priorities and performance issues within the business areas it supports.

The Goal and Initiatives layer for an enterprise aims to improve and provide understanding of the drivers, objectives and initiatives the enterprise has established or is setting itself, and to which the IT organisation needs to respond.

For the EA function, this means defining the purpose for which the EA exists (the mission statement) and what kind of EA function it intends to be (the vision statement). Given this mission and vision, it is important to then ask what are the primary goals of the EA function and when will it know that it has successfully achieved or progressed towards these goals (its outcome measures).

What is the concept of operations for the EA function?

A concept of operations is a non-technical, high level description of the enterprise being undertaken, and is used to help communicate and achieve agreement on the scope and intent of the enterprise that key stakeholders endorse.

The concept of operations for the EA function is based on the assumption that corporate and IT governance functions will improve planning and oversight and make better decisions if there is clear, consistent, accessible and useful information about an enterprise's current and future architecture. It also requires that an agreed plan to transition between the two has been developed from an integrated strategic, business and technology perspective.

This concept is illustrated in Figure 4, where EA is shown as part of an integrated approach to governance, represented by the hub and spokes, and responsible for managing the enterprise's strategic, business and technology data in a manner that will support the other governance functions and management processes decision-making, represented by the framework.

Figure 4: Concept of Operations for the EA function (Artefact S-3)

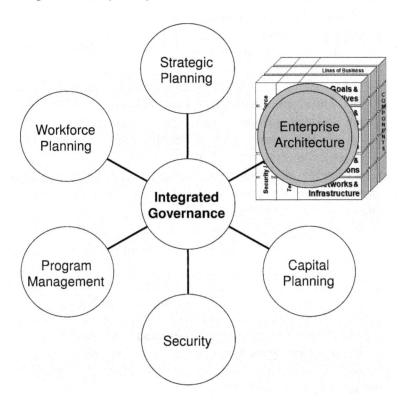

What is a potential future operating scenario for the EA function?

Seeking early clarification of the type of enterprise being envisioned and the capabilities necessary to support the enterprise helps explain the mission and vision in non-technical terms, focuses documentation and assessment efforts and encourages stakeholder involvement and buy in.

Described in terms of a future operating scenario, the table below describes the future operating model for the EA function that focuses on the key governance interactions outlined above and that is being promoted within the reference architecture. A brief description of the key planning assumptions required for the processes, people, and technology to support and implement the operating model are also provided. These highlight the key enablers and introduce the key components that need to be 'fleshed out' in the other layers of the EA function.

Table 1: Future Operating Scenario for the EA function (Artefact S-3)

	Planning Assumptions
The strategic planning function division is currently undertaking its annual strategic planning review and update of its 3-year plan.	
Referring to the Enterprise Architecture (EA) portal, the strategic planners walk through a list of last year's drivers. Meetings with senior executives and an analysis of the market identifies that a major change initiative is required to address a change in a major competitor's position.	**Process:** EA is a recognised part of the organisation's governance community. **People**: EA team is suitably skilled to input to the strategic planning process. **Technology**: The EA repository presents key strategic elements, influences, goals, objectives, strategies, tactics, etc.
From the EA portal the strategic planners list the strategies that were agreed on last year, and review the associated business activities that were involved and affected and the owning organisational units responsible for the business functions.	**Process:** EA is the accepted method of consistently documenting the different lines of business. **Technology**: The EA repository reflects the relationship between strategic elements and business activities.
Meetings are organised within each of the responsible organisational units. The meetings include the Enterprise Business Architect (s) in order for management to understand the current state and external and internal influences affecting the organisation. During each meeting, referring to documentation extracted from the EA portal that outlines the information requirements and improvements and proposed IT solutions to meet these, progress against plan is reviewed and	**People:** EA Business Architects are recognised as the single point of contact responsible for the consistent documentation of all business units' key internal influences. **Technology**: Views of the business activities and key information flows suitable for planning discussions are maintained and readily available.

Planning Assumptions

changes and new priorities identified where appropriate.

Discussions confirm that progress against plan is generally going well across all business units. One organisational unit, however, identified that a regulatory requirement has recently been introduced requiring their urgent attention. The Enterprise Business Architect is tasked with documenting the changes in priorities.

The strategic planners then organise a meeting with the Chief Architect and Enterprise Technology Architects to discuss the current position in relation to data, application and technology components.

Process: The EA team is seen as a trusted partner in the alignment of business and IT priorities.

People: The EA team consists of members with business and IT strategy and planning experience.

In collaboration, throughout the year, the IT organisation and the Enterprise Architecture teams have systematically identified and reviewed various components within the technology architecture based on problems encountered, operating cost reviews and new information that has come to hand regarding developments in the broader IT industry. From this, a number of potential strategic and tactical initiatives have been identified. These are presented and discussed with the strategic planners.

Process: The IT organisation uses the EA function as a single point of coordination and/or capture of issues, plans and positions associated with technology components.

Technology: On behalf of IT, the repository captures and documents relevant plans, positions, standards and principles in place and for consideration.

In particular, it has been determined that single sign-on (SSO) technology has reached a point of maturity and integration making it feasible to phase out current solutions, greatly enhance users' experience with technology and reduce IT cost and complexity.

Process: EA performs documentation and assessment 'deep dives' on specific business, enterprise or technical service areas to further help decision-making.

Planning Assumptions

Using the available external and internal information that the strategic planners have collected from their own analysis and discussions with the business and IT personnel, senior management agree on a modified plan of action focusing on identifying and selling higher value products, addressing the regulatory concern and improving productivity through more seamless access between its applications.

Technology: The current strategic plan is published to the enterprise, and in a form that is suitable for subsequent planning activities.

Line of business managers are asked to review their operations in light of the agreed strategic plan and formulate their course of action for the year. In conjunction with their Enterprise Business Architect, each line of business reviews the details of the strategic plan, highlighting gaps between their current operating models and the new strategic plan, and performance issues impacting their current operating model.

Technology: For each line of business, the current operating model is documented and presentable in a form that simplifies gap identification (including new requirements specification) and process and resources where performance issues occur, and facilitates their sharing, review and understanding.

Reviews, budgetary discussions and planning sessions are conducted to help firm-up the changes required in each line of business that will help meet strategic requirements and performance issues. Opportunities for Lines of business to: achieve quick wins due to plans in other parts of the business; gain advantage from economies of scale due to overlapping requirements; promote their responsibilities; and firm up their role as part of enterprise are discussed and considered by reviewing the current and planned changes and requirements for services and components across the enterprise.

Technology: Details of each line of business service requirements and changes as part of their future operating model are published facilitating identification of potential overlapping impacts and requirements.

Planning Assumptions

In light of the strategic plan, business plans and IT strategies and tactics, the EA team is asked to formulate the set of high level solutions and transition plan that takes into consideration the current IT principles, standards and dependencies and business and IT budgets and priorities. Working with representatives from the business (with a good understanding of the service requirements and changes) and from IT (with a good understanding of the technical considerations of each high level solution), a portfolio of work, and related future business and IT models, are proposed.

Process: EA is responsible for developing the EA management plan outlining the high level changes to the IT architecture to support the strategic and business requirements within and across the lines of business.

Process: The EA management plan is part of the annual planning cycle.

People: The EA team has EA development and IT solutions skills.

Technology: Views of the IT principles, standards and dependencies, and business and IT budgets and priorities suitable for planning discussions are maintained and readily available.

The regulatory project and the single sign-on project commence at approximately the same time. The implementation of each project, from initiation through to deployment and associated change management activities, has been outsourced to different consulting organisations. Each of the project teams review the business and technical services associated with their project, with team members concentrating on the rationale for the changes, the gaps between the current and future business and technical models, and the dependencies, principles and standards, etc. that are relevant to their role within the project. They direct any questions to the EA team for clarification.

Process: EA is the accepted method of reducing misinterpretation and improving communications of the change requirements, outcomes, etc. that were agreed in response to the strategic, business and technology plans.

People: The EA team is responsible for helping to communicate and clarify the changes, standards, plans, etc. within the EA

Technology: The EA management plan and associated artefacts and various management views targeted at different roles within project teams are usable and accessible.

	Planning Assumptions

Over the course of a few months, business and IT solution designs are put forward, the EA team is consulted to assess the proposed changes and requirements against the portfolio of work and against the future business and IT models and principles and standards, highlighting areas of divergence and recommending whether the solution needs further work, or determining whether the architecture needs updating to reflect any new realities. Where insufficient information is known within the EA, the EA team defer to its relevant business and IT representatives and SMEs for more information.

Process: EA is expected to verify conformance and alignment with principles, directions, plans, etc. that were agreed within the EA management plan.

People: The EA team has sufficient capacity to review and assess business cases and solution designs.

People: Domain experts and representatives are identified and enabled to provide input to the EA.

Technology: The ability to track and document conformance and variations of solutions to the EA.

The two projects are cutover into production, changing the enterprise's strategic, business and existing technology architecture. The EA team updates the current state artefacts to reflect these changes, and future state and transition plan artefacts to reflect attainment of input objectives.

Process: EA is notified of changes to the actual architecture.

What is the vision and mission of the EA function?

Based on the above concept of operations and future operating scenario, the mission and vision for the EA function is listed in Table 2.

Table 2: Mission and Vision for the EA function (Artefact - S-1)

Mission	To analyse and document the enterprise in its current and future state from a strategy, business and technology (SB&T) perspective.
Vision	To improve (enterprise and) IT planning, and change oversight and decision-making through good, right and successful[2] enterprise architecture.

[2] Good - architecturally sound, Right - meets the goals of its stakeholders and Successful – attributed with substantial business success. – (CC-Great EA)

The mission outlines the means by which the EA function will endeavour to achieve the vision of improving the performance of the related governance functions and management processes it aims to service.

Specifically, the EA function being espoused will:

- Analyse as well as document the enterprise in both its current form and the agreed target form to achieve the vision
- Consider drivers, imperatives, etc. from a strategic level to help ensure decisions take into account new directions the enterprise may need to take, key process and performance issues from a business perspective to ensure they too are addressed, and technology changes and trends to ensure technical considerations are duly evaluated and tactical IT issues addressed.

The primary results of undertaking the above must be improvements to the abilities of related and/or integrated governance functions and management processes to identify, prioritise, plan, implement and track IT-related changes to the enterprise.

Who are the beneficiaries of right, good and successful EA?

All enterprises, whether they be a private organisation selling products or services; a government agency delivering services to citizens; or a business unit, function or capability internal to an organisation, have people other than just their customers who benefit from their sale or delivery of products or services. That is, those with a vested interest in the success of the enterprise and who are the key sources of information and influence on the scope and intent of the enterprise.

For the EA function, those with a vested interest are those roles and positions internal and external to the enterprise that will benefit from the improvements brought about from good, right and successful EA.

The principal stakeholders for the type of EA espoused by the reference architecture are listed in Table 3.

Table 3: EA Stakeholders (Artefact S-1)

Stakeholder	Description
The Executive	The Executive has a vested interest in EA due to its ability to help plan and communicate the initiatives necessary to support any changes in direction, and to answer why the changes are, or were, necessary.

Stakeholder	Description
Lines of Business Owners	Lines of Business Owners have a vested interest in EA as it provides another means of having their business changes and performance priorities considered and met.
Chief Information Officer (CIO)	CIOs are stakeholders of EA as they benefit from greater visibility of the strategic and business drivers and requirements, the ability to identify cross-enterprise reuse and redundancy elimination opportunities, and more accurate alignment of their operations to support business needs.

To deliver the benefits of EA to whom are the EA function's products and services provided?

Customers of an enterprise are the beneficiaries of the products and services of the enterprise. The type and needs of customers fulfilled and targeted by an enterprise are a significant input to the capabilities requirements of the enterprise.

Based on the concept of operations and the mission and vision of the reference architecture EA function, the customers of EA are those that will use EA information and services to support or help decision-making in pursuit of their own functional and governance responsibilities.

For example, Workforce Planners have a planning responsibility within the broader enterprise. Through better information about the future skill and knowledge requirements of new or changed business and technology activities and resources, Workforce Planners can make more timely and accurate recruitment and training-related decisions and plans.

Described as actors on a system context diagram, Figure 5 illustrates the range of roles across the various business and IT governance functions and management processes typically responsible for enterprise and IT planning, oversight and decision-making that the EA function can and should treat as its customers. Each of the EA customers' concerns and governance responsibilities are listed in Table 4 to help describe the type of decision-making that the reference architecture EA function should aim to improve.

Figure 5: EA Customers (Artefact S-1)

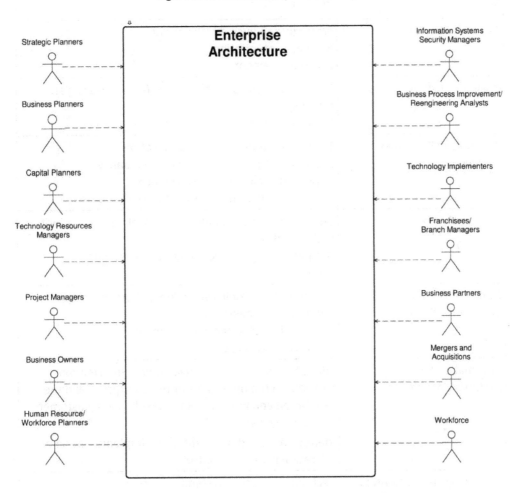

Table 4: EA Customers and Responsibilities (Artefact S-1)

EA Customers	Responsibilities
Capital Planners	Enterprise-level investment portfolio optimisation Business cases accurately reflect priorities and opportunities Business change delivery focus is maintained and proportionate Business change delivers the expected returns
Strategic Planners	Shareholder satisfaction, for whom do we do it? Enterprise positioning and direction, what do we do? Business transformation alignment, how do we excel?

EA Customers	Responsibilities
Business Planners	Strategic and business alignment Business optimisation Risk management
Business Owners	Managing business performance (i.e. measuring and tracking) Overseeing changes to business operations
Technology Resources Managers	Technology reuse and standardisation Removing unplanned or costly redundancy Improving technology performance Timely and cost-effective support of IT solutions
Project Managers	Business case development accurately reflects priority and opportunity Business change delivery focus is maintained and proportionate
Human Resource/ Workforce Planners	Induction and training selection and provisioning Retention management Individuals performance assessment Employee satisfaction
Information Systems Security Managers	Identification of risks associated with Information Systems on the operations of the enterprise, and the reputation and interests of its stakeholders, customers and employees. Identification and oversight of the implementation of migration plans and controls.
Technology Implementers	Technology reuse and standardisation Timely and cost-effective delivery and support of IT solutions
Business Process Improvement/Reengineering Analysts	Business process performance improvement Business process optimisation Business process standardisation
Business Partners	Service level delivery Mutual advantage to enterprise and self
Franchisees/Branch Managers	Required activities and resources Head office integration
Mergers and Acquisitions	Fit to current architecture Effort to integrate Ease of assessment
Workforce	Operational execution Personal measures

What are the drivers and mandates that influence EA that need to be addressed?

Understanding and assessing the capabilities of an enterprise is one of first steps of any strategic planning activity. This involves reviewing the environment (external influences) in which the enterprise operates and the suitability and performance of the capabilities within the enterprise (internal influences).

One method of assessing and documenting influences on an enterprise is the SWOT analysis method. The influences are classified according to whether they are internal and can be leveraged, and therefore a strength; internal and need to be resolved or mitigated, and therefore a weakness; external and can be used to benefit the enterprise, therefore an opportunity; or external and likely to impact the position or operations of the enterprise, and therefore a threat.

In Table 5 are listed a number of influences typical for EA based on the experiences and learnings of EA practitioners, over a period of two decades, that have helped to shape and determine the degree of success. They cover a range of factors internal and external to the EA function that commonly need to be addressed by an organisation when establishing or operating an EA function. In summary they cover such themes as:

- The increasing demand for readily-accessible, secure, accurate and complete information and knowledge to support fact- or evidence-based decision-making
- The ongoing problem of optimising IT investments with strategic and business drivers
- The continued divergence and increasing complexity of IT
- The risks associated with starting up and running non-core management disciplines, which EA still tends to be classified as
- The common causes of failure of relatively new and/or immature disciplines, which EA is often considered
- Leveraging existing or available knowledge and skills effectively.

Table 5: EA Function Influences (Artefact S-2)

Influence	Type	Description / Rationale	Source
Existing IT Governance Functions	Strength	Existing governance functions/management processes provide a ready source of planning, decision-making and oversight requirements and an existing structure with which to design the	

Influence	Type	Description / Rationale	Source
		future integration points for the EA function.	
Existing Sub-Architecture Information	Strength	Use and availability of existing artefacts can significantly reduce the effort required to centralise and share knowledge about the enterprise, to learn about and assess the enterprise and to determine documentation standards for future initiatives.	
Existing Sub-Architecture Skills	Strength	The greater the level of knowledge, skill and experience available in an organisation in sub-architecture areas and best practices, the more straightforward is the assessment and design of these elements within an EA context.	
Architecture Scope Is Too Big	3Weakness	One of the most difficult aspects when starting or reviving an EA program is determining the appropriate scope level. The early EA efforts have to be significant enough to acquire the big picture view of the organisation and deliver value. By wanting to make sure that the EA Program delivers value, many organisations make the mistake of selecting an initial architecture scope that is too large.	NFAEAAP, 2009
Insufficient Resources	Weakness	As a corporate initiative, it is important to recognise not only the direct expenses such as funding the Chief Architect and the EA Office, but also the non-direct expenses related to governance, project managers, and designers and developers who apply their work to conforming to the EA. Even when organisations have the proper holistic outlook for their EA Program, there is no guarantee that the program will receive adequate funding, especially during periods of economic stricture.	CSFEAE, 2007
Loss Of Key Personnel	Weakness	EA is an emerging area of professional practice that requires management, sponsorship, business representation, architects, analysts, developers, and programmers. Each of these skill sets is	NFAEAAP, 2009

Influence	Type	Description / Rationale	Source
		important to the program, and the loss of members of the EA team with those skills can create delays in program implementation, as well as effect implementation costs.	
New/Inadequate Technology - EA Tools	Weakness	One of the greatest challenges for a Chief Architect is to develop current and future views of the EA that are rich in detail and easy to access, and which can support modelling and decision-making types of queries. The capabilities of EA tools and supporting applications at present are such that intuitive and informative management views of EA information are difficult to produce. Because more than one software application is normally required in an EA program, tool integration is an issue that must also be dealt with.	NFAEAAP, 2009
Unclear Leadership	Weakness	Lack of clear leadership is a major factor in EA Program failure. In fact, the 2006 GAO report indicates that getting senior level support was seen as a challenge by nearly 50% of all agencies.	NFAEAAP, 2009
Unclear View Of Mission Services	Weakness	Lack of a clear definition of the services that an EA function or the Enterprise Architects will provide, and the capability required to deliver these, often results in Enterprise Architects being used for a broad range of technology and solution activities, confusing and bringing into question the purpose, value and type of resource required for EA.	
Different Answers Given For The Same Questions	Opportunity	When an internal or external customer asks for information, the answer they are provided is often different depending on who they asked, or the source they refer to. This problem suggests siloed, duplicated data and/or poor information sharing.	EAaS, 2006
Different Processes Completing The	Opportunity	As a result of siloed business planning, mergers and acquisitions, tactical requirements and implementations, etc.	EAaS, 2006

Influence	Type	Description / Rationale	Source
Same Activity with Different Systems		businesses can wittingly or unwittingly end up performing the same type of activities using different people, processes and technology across the business. Examples include payments processing, project management, IT support, data management, etc. This can negatively affect a business through inconsistent delivery of services, increased compliance and training costs, divergent technology solutions, etc. EA can help in this situation by highlighting all types of duplicate activities and prioritising opportunities to rationalise, consolidate or standardise these activities.	
IT Is Consistently A Bottleneck	Opportunity	An IT department struggling to deliver on IT performance improvements and requirements, while still busy supporting and maintaining, may be indicative of an overly-complex IT environment and/or poorly focused portfolio of work.	EAaS, 2006
Information For Key Decisions Is Not Available	Opportunity	Difficulties in making sound decisions about process and resource changes typically indicates the lack of an integrated approach to managing and communicating the relationships, dependencies and inherent priorities between strategy, business and technology.	EAaS, 2006
Meeting A New Regulation Is Hard	Opportunity	The absence of existing line of sight from strategy through business and to technology, and/or existing models to facilitate communications and impact assessment, requires substantial effort to rediscover information necessary to make informed and accurate implementation decisions.	EAaS, 2006
Senior Management Dreads IT Meetings	Opportunity	Avoidance or poor engagement of IT by management and other functional areas of the business is commonly the result of poorly understood or irrelevant technology solutions being put forward; a perception that IT is unable to support or contribute	EAaS, 2006

Influence	Type	Description / Rationale	Source
		to strategic or business improvement programs; and/or a poor track record in the delivery of the IT component of change programs. The key means by which EA can help under this scenario is by pitching changes in terms of the processes, activities and information flows familiar to and used by management and the non-IT functional areas, and balancing/aligning the strategic, business and technology plans.	
Significant Work Activity Around Moving Information From One System To Another	Opportunity	Reliance on double entry and difficulty integrating systems is often symptomatic of an IT environment with both duplicate data across its systems and/or non-standard systems not geared towards interoperability.	EAaS, 2006
Strategic Initiative Is Like Starting From Scratch	Opportunity	The absence of existing line of sight from strategy through business and to technology, and/or existing models to facilitate communications and impact assessment, requires substantial effort to rediscover information necessary to make informed and accurate implementation decisions.	EAaS, 2006
Competition With Other Best Practices	Threat	It is not uncommon for business and IT leaders to latch onto today's 'hottest' industry trends or best practices in an effort to keep an equal footing with their competitors. There are several best practice programs that could aid an organisation, yet none of those can deliver all the benefits that a successful EA Program can. Examples of perceived alternatives/competitors include ITIL, Business Process Reengineering/Management and Six Sigma.	jEA-200905
Lack Of Perceived Value	Threat	A very significant challenge to establishing a right, good and successful EA Program, and a frequent reason why EA Programs	NFAEAAP, 2009

Influence	Type	Description / Rationale	Source
		fail, is the lack of perceived value from EA within the organisation.	
Lack Of Use	Threat	A key reason why EA Programs fail is the inability to use the architecture effectively once it has been developed. Many early EA efforts are detoured awaiting approval of their first deliverable.	NFAEAAP, 2009
Not Sure If Good Value Is Coming From IT	Threat	An IT department struggling to deliver on IT performance improvements and requirements, while still busy supporting and maintaining, may be indicative of an overly-complex IT environment and/or poorly focused portfolio of work.	EAaS, 2006
Not Understanding EA Is And Is Not	Threat	Perhaps one of the greatest challenges to establishing a successful EA Program, and by extension a re-launched effort, is that there are tremendous misconceptions as to what EA actually encompasses.	NFAEAAP, 2009

What targets should the EA program aim for if it is to deliver a right, good and successful EA function?

Once the drivers and mandates on the enterprise are understood, analysed and prioritised, an enterprise needs to determine where to focus its attention.

One method of describing the targets of an enterprise is Kaplan and Norton's Balanced Scorecard approach to strategy development. One of the main principles of the Balanced Scorecard approach is that an enterprise's directions and focus are most effectively set, balanced and explained when considered from four perspectives:

1. *Financial, or Shareholder, perspective*
2. *Customer perspective*
3. *Internal Process, and activities, perspective*
4. *Learning and Growth perspective, which covers the people (referred to as the human capital), technology (referred to as information capital), and organisational enablers.*

For the EA function these four perspectives are equivalent to:

1. The EA stakeholders, i.e. executives, managers and technical people, requiring changes to the enterprise to meet strategic and business priorities.

2. The EA customers who will benefit directly from integration with an EA capability, as it will allow them to better plan and oversee changes required to help attain the EA stakeholders' required outcomes.
3. The services and activities the EA function provides and performs to meet its customers' requirements, and to ensure it manages an effective and sustainable function.
4. The people, technology and organisational inputs required to effectively enable the EA services and activity delivery.

Described in terms of a Balanced Scorecard Strategy Map, Figure 6 illustrates the types of objectives an EA function should strive for across the four perspectives. Each of the business objectives is described, and the types of measures that could be used to track progress and to quantify value to the enterprise are listed in Table 6.

Figure 6: A Balanced Scorecard Strategy Map for the EA function (Artefact S-5)

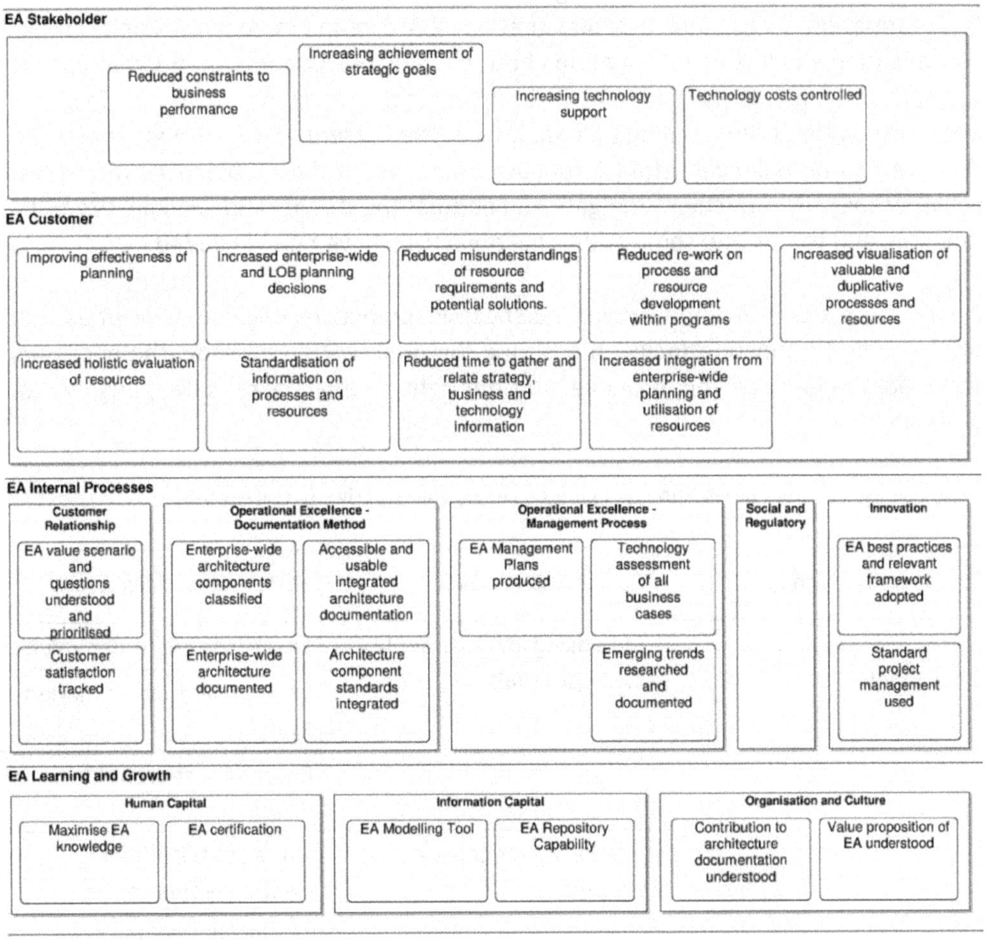

EA Stakeholder

Reduced constraints to business performance	Increasing achievement of strategic goals	
	Increasing technology support	Technology costs controlled

EA Customer

Improving effectiveness of planning	Increased enterprise-wide and LOB planning decisions	Reduced misunderstandings of resource requirements and potential solutions.	Reduced re-work on process and resource development within programs	Increased visualisation of valuable and duplicative processes and resources
Increased holistic evaluation of resources	Standardisation of information on processes and resources	Reduced time to gather and relate strategy, business and technology information	Increased integration from enterprise-wide planning and utilisation of resources	

EA Internal Processes

Customer Relationship	Operational Excellence - Documentation Method		Operational Excellence - Management Process		Social and Regulatory	Innovation
EA value scenario and questions understood and prioritised	Enterprise-wide architecture components classified	Accessible and usable integrated architecture documentation	EA Management Plans produced	Technology assessment of all business cases		EA best practices and relevant framework adopted
Customer satisfaction tracked	Enterprise-wide architecture documented	Architecture component standards integrated		Emerging trends researched and documented		Standard project management used

EA Learning and Growth

Human Capital		Information Capital		Organisation and Culture	
Maximise EA knowledge	EA certification	EA Modelling Tool	EA Repository Capability	Contribution to architecture documentation understood	Value proposition of EA understood

In the first level are four objectives representing the key value propositions that improved governance brought about by EA should ultimately achieve (FUN, EATP). In brief, they equate to the business and IT transformations and efficiency improvements sought by most organisations.

From a Customer perspective the objectives of the EA effort are to benefit its customers by delivering services in line with the EA function's concept of operations and vision and mission. Several objectives are provided that directly relate to planning and oversight decision-making improvements. These can and should be brought about by improving access to usable information about the current and future architectures of the enterprise from an integrated strategy, business and technology perspective (AIEA, 2005).

From an Internal Process perspective, the intent is to focus the EA on excelling at establishing and managing the core elements of the proposed approach to EA, and performance of the documentation and management activities that will deliver the EA information access and usability that the EA customers require. For example, consolidating and linking information about changeable EA components that are the subject of investments and classification of the EA components to facilitate enterprise-wide understanding and analysis of the current and future architectures. However, to be balanced, the EA function must also include objectives to address activities that will proactively mitigate and address the threats and weaknesses of the function, and to this end some additional objectives have been included.

Finally, from a Learning and Growth perspective, objectives have been included that will help the EA function focus on ensuring the organisation is ready, the necessary technology is in place and available, and the right people are recruited, engaged or up-skilled :

Table 6: EA Function Objectives by Perspective (Artefact S-5)

Perspective	Group	Business Objective	Performance Measures
EA Stakeholder		Increasing achievement of strategic goals	Enterprise customer value
			Enterprise product market size
			Enterprise shareholder value
		Increasing technology support	Greater utilisation of existing technologies
			Fewer information flow-related performance issues

Perspective	Group	Business Objective	Performance Measures
		Reduced constraints to business performance	Reduce gaps in LOB performance
			Reduced duplicated or stove-piped resources
			Improved support for BP management/reengineering activities
		Technology costs controlled	Technology costs in line with benchmarks and strategic directions
			Average number of technologies against technical services
EA Customer		Improving effectiveness of planning	Reduced capital planning time
			Improved capital planning effectiveness
		Increased enterprise-wide and LOB planning decisions	Cross-segment processes and resources
			Requests for enterprise-wide processes and resource opportunities
		Increased holistic evaluation of resources	Investments originating from EA Management Plan
			Duplicative processes and resources
		Increased integration from enterprise-wide planning and utilisation of resources	Cross-segment processes and resources
		Increased visualisation of valuable and duplicative processes and resources	EA components classified
		Reduced misunderstandings of resource requirements and potential solutions.	Project scope changes
			Solution architecture effort
		Reduced re-work on process and resource development within programs	Duplicative processes and resources
			Solution architecture effort

Perspective	Group	Business Objective	Performance Measures
			Investments originating from EA Management Plan
		Reduced time to gather and relate strategy, business and technology information	Solution architecture effort
		Standardisation of information on processes and resources	Reduced number of architecture documentation methods and repositories
EA Internal Processes	Customer Relationship	Customer satisfaction tracked	EA Customer satisfaction
		EA value scenario and questions understood and prioritised	Perceived value of contribution to EA customer function
	Innovation	EA best practices and relevant framework adopted	Effort to familiarise to new process
		Standard project management used	Agreed and managed program of EA work
	Operational Excellence - Documentation Method	Accessible and usable integrated architecture documentation	Amount of access and usage
			EA questions answerable directly or otherwise
		Architecture component standards integrated	Artefact standards centrally accessible
		Enterprise-wide architecture components classified	Architecture component reference models
		Enterprise-wide architecture documented	Segments documented consistently
	Operational Excellence - Management Process	EA Management Plans produced	Enterprise customer value
			Enterprise product market size
			Enterprise shareholder value
		Emerging trends researched and documented	Accuracy and completeness of trends
		Technology assessment of all business cases	Investments architecturally reviewed.

Perspective	Group	Business Objective	Performance Measures
EA Learning and Growth	Human Capital	EA certification	EAs Certified
		Maximise EA knowledge	Staff knowledge of Strategy, Business & Technology drivers and concepts
			Staff knowledge about EA Elements
	Information Capital	EA Modelling Tool	Procured and Installed
			Effort required to extend
		EA Repository Capability	Procured and Installed
			Effort required to extend
	Organisation and Culture	Contribution to architecture documentation understood	Willingness of SME to be available
		Value proposition of EA understood	Executive and Management Briefs

To understand which influences each business objective was included to address, refer to the Appendix - Business Objective to Influence Mappings.

What should be considered when documenting and analysing the Goals and Initiatives Layer?

For an Enterprise

When documenting and assessing the Goals and Initiative layer of the enterprise, the following are likely to need consideration:

1. **What are the boundaries/scope of the enterprise?**

   An enterprise may be small like an EA function, an organisational unit like IT or Human Resources, an organisation, or a combination of organisations. An organisation may limit the size of an enterprise for multiple reasons:

   o Time constraints. The greater the size of an enterprise the more the stakeholders, components, relationships, etc. are required to be documented and analysed.
   o Priorities. Based on past investments, current influences, people dynamics, etc. one area of an organisation may require greater planning and oversight decision-support than another.

    ○   Budget. EA, like any other program, must compete for funding. The larger the enterprise the greater the budget required to achieve the same level of rigour, value, detail, etc.

2. **Who is responsible for determining the goals and initiatives of the enterprise?**

As the enterprise broadens or goes up the organisational chart, the greater the chance and likelihood of the development and specification of the goals and initiatives to be the responsibility of another department, management process or governance function. As this becomes the case, the EA function will become more responsible for collating and understanding the goals and initiatives rather than influencing or setting them. The practises and methods used for deriving and documenting the components of the goals and initiatives are also likely to have been already set.

3. **Which goals and initiatives?**

Not all strategic or corporate goals and initiatives apply to the products and services in scope of the enterprise. Analysis of the goals and initiatives will identify some more relevant than others. Focusing on analysing, documenting and linking to only these reduces the effort and quantity of documentation to be managed and maintained.

4. **Business or IT planner?**

EA grew out of attempts to improve business and IT alignment. The need to understand the strategic level or corporate goals and initiatives arose to help identify the drivers for changes to the IT architecture.

EA, however, is increasingly seen as a method that can also help define the business architecture upon which business plans can be based. Under this scenario, all the strategic or corporate goals and initiatives across all the products and services that are in scope of the enterprise need to be analysed, documented and linked, and the business priorities and performance issues, whether or not related to IT also need to be covered.

This will ensure that EA, according to its broadest definition and, some would say its underlying intent, is being performed, and that it equally contributes to the development and oversight of business and IT plans.

For the EA Function

When documenting and assessing the EA function's Goals and Initiatives layer, consider the following:

1. **Develop the Future Operating Scenario**

    The future operating scenario for the EA function helps to communicate and agree the scope and intent of the EA function in a non-technical and easily-understood and clear manner. The one provided above covers the full scope and intent of the reference architecture EA. Add or remove sections, rename actors, processes and resources to align with your organisation and socialise and refine. Be sure to identify the planning assumptions as the first method of assessing the current state of your EA function.

2. **Review the Influences**

    The influences supplied above provide good coverage of the key internal and external influences that are typically confronted by an EA function. Consider each for relevance to your organisation, and score and prioritise accordingly as a second method of assessing the current state of your EA function and identifying what is currently important to the broader organisation.

3. **Draft the Strategic Objectives for the EA function**

    One of the objectives identified above for operational excellence is the management process side of EA, which requires having a good, clear and accurate description of the current state, and the plans and targets for the EA function itself; that is, an EA for the EA function. First time through the production of the EA for the EA function, however, no EA exists. In fact, in most organisations, no EA ever exists for their EA function, or for any governance function for that matter. The most common method to address this gap is through the use of assessment frameworks, or the like.

    Several assessment frameworks exist to help organisations to assess the current state of their EA function and highlight priority areas and targets. To accompany EA[3], Dr Bernard has developed the EA Audit Framework, refer to Appendix - EA Audit Model (EA2M) for details. The EA2M framework is particularly appropriate because:

    o   The Utilisation audit category covers and helps focus the goal and initiative-setting of components in the strategy layer of the EA[3] framework, by focusing on the assessment of such things as EA customers, what services are needed, and what targets we have

o The areas in the Completeness and Consistency audit categories cover and help focus goal and initiative-setting for the business and technology layers, and common threads within the EA^3 framework, by focusing the assessment on the EA^3 core elements such as Integrated Governance, Methodology, Tools and Repository and Training.

Use EA2M as a third method of assessing the current state of your EA function.

4. Draft the Strategic Performance Measures

The EA function business objectives described earlier in this section were identified to help achieve a balanced EA function that is aligned with the reference architecture-defined mission and vision.

Using the results of the previous three steps, rank and set the performance measures for each business objective. Business objectives that address higher priority influences, or that align with more important business needs will obviously be given more attention as part of the EA program. However, lower priority business objectives should not be ignored or de-scoped as this will 'unbalance' the EA function.

5. Socialise the Strategic Objectives and Targets

Refine the objectives and targets with the EA stakeholders to help direct and confirm EA function priorities and to help reflect attainment of each of the business objectives over time.

6. Refine Business and Technology Objectives

Continue to update the business objectives in the bottom two perspectives of the Balanced Scorecard in response to assessments performed during the lower layers of the EA framework.

Section 2 – The Products and Services of the EA function

Once directions and priorities have been set for an enterprise, analysing and describing the changes to the products and services to be delivered must be finalised. This will require the business capabilities necessary to deliver these products and services, described in unambiguous terms familiar to their owners, and sufficiently detailed to derive and define information requirements.

This is the first step in bridging the gap between strategy and implementation, and describing strategy in a meaningful way to each of the principals involved in planning and implementation of change.

From an EA perspective, this layer of the Reference Architecture focuses on describing the future business of doing EA. In this layer, the requirements of the EA function to be met are fleshed out, and the products, services and activities to be established to meet the requirements are described.

In keeping with the concept of operations and the vision and mission of the EA function, the EA function must provide services that will assist its customers to perform their own governance functions more effectively. That is, the services that will improve the access to, and usefulness of, the information about an enterprise's architecture. Specifically, the services must target the information requirements of individual roles within the organisation's governance functions and management processes.

The activities/processes of the EA function that need to be established include not only the delivery of the services, but also the additional activities necessary to plan and manage the EA function, formalise and establish the elements of the approach, and develop, integrate and assure the contents of the architectures.

What are the key requirements of the EA function's products and services?

A good understanding of the target market for any enterprise is essential to its products and services delivering value or benefit to its customers, or recipients of its services. This requires insights into the problems, needs and desires of the customers.

The principal customers of EA are the other governance functions and management processes responsible for the planning and implementation of change. In principle, EA is meant to help them do their work better by providing integrated information about the enterprise in its current and future states, and the transitional activities necessary to move between the two.

During planning, understanding current issues, dependencies and standards helps to prioritise and define change quicker, more accurately and with greater consistency. During implementation, understanding what changes are being made, why they are required and how they fit together or contribute to the whole, helps avoid divergence, waste and misinterpretation.

These requirements of the governance functions and management processes are best described as the queries about the architecture of the enterprise that will support their particular decision-making responsibilities. That is, the relevant information about the current state of the changeable components within the enterprise, the new components, new component guidelines and changes to existing components that will make up the future enterprise, and the investments and sequence plan to affect the transition.

A representative set of these queries is listed, in Table 7. Queries are listed against the governance functions and management processes defined earlier in the Goals and Initiatives layer, referred to as EA customers, which they are most likely to be asked by.

The queries are described in terms of the architectural documentation and data an EA can be expected to manage and use in keeping with the scope and intent of the reference architecture EA. That is, the EA layers cover many components whose specific information management, storage and usage responsibilities belong to other governance functions. EA is not intended to replace these responsibilities, only to provide a view of these components in an integrated, accessible and useful way that will improve planning and oversight decision-making within and between governance functions and management processes with which the EA function is integrated, and not trying to answer all potential questions about components in the enterprise.

Table 7: EA Customer Architectural Questions (Artefact B-1)

EA Customer	Concerns and Questions
Capital Planners	What opportunities are there to consolidate process and resources across LOBs?
	How is the business and IT spend aligned to the strategic directions?
	What projects should be prioritised from an expenditure perspective?
	Where are there potential overlaps in scope between projects/programs of work?
	Does a project take into account all the business functions that it should?
	Where are we focusing our investments (active and proposed)?
	How are our investments aligned to our corporate strategic direction?
	What are our priorities for focusing investments and effort?
	What are the cross-divisional considerations and dependencies of the project?
Strategic Planners	How is the business and IT spend aligned to the strategic directions?
	How can we support better alignment across the transformation and support plans?
	How are the capabilities of the enterprise positioned to support new directions?
	Where are we focusing our investments (active and proposed)?
	How are our investments aligned to our corporate strategic direction?
	What components of our business are required to support a market opportunity?
	How can I assess what I can leverage to exploit potential market opportunities?
	What pipeline activity would support a particular new product or market?
	What internal business services could be leveraged as an external offering?
	What opportunities/alternative models exist for delivering a service?

EA Customer	Concerns and Questions
	How do I compare the enterprise's performance to other organisations/competitors?
	What does it cost to deliver a particular business function?
	What are the current 'pain points' for my Line of Business?
	What are the impacts if a new market or product/service offering is pursued?
	How do we as an organisation deliver products and services to customers?
	What are our priorities for focusing investments and effort?
Business Planners	What business activities support strategic direction and business priorities?
	What are the strategic drivers and directions of the enterprise/segment?
	What are the business activities identified to support the strategic drivers?
	What is the current transition plan for my line of business?
	What business activities within a line of business remain unimplemented?
	What performance issues are associated with activities within an LOB?
	What business activities are duplicated across lines of business?
	What information flow and data transformations does the knowledge plan support?
Business Owners	What is the current transition plan/investments for my line of business?
	What business activities support strategic direction and business priorities?
	What performance measures are associated with business activities?
	What information flow and transformation requirements of new activities?
	What produces or consumes the information flows of required business activities?
	What information flow changes are associated with the business activities?
	How effective have executed investments been?

EA Customer	Concerns and Questions
Technology Resource Managers	Where are the opportunities for replacing or decommissioning IT systems?
	Which LOBs have a large number of applications (and interfaces)?
	Where are there potential overlaps in application capability/system functions?
	What business activities are impacted by a decision to invest in a technology?
	What are the knowledge and skill areas for a particular technology/application?
	What business activities are being supported by a particular technology?
Project Managers	How is my investment aligned to our corporate strategic direction?
	Where are there potential overlaps in scope between projects/programs of work?
	Does a project take into account all the business functions that it should?
	What are the projects' cross-LOB considerations and dependencies?
	What are the business activities within scope of my project?
	What should my project be including in its scope?
	What other projects affect the same processes and resources my project will?
	How do I understand and reflect the impact of a change request on my project?
	What are the future EA components delivered and changed by this project?
	What business services or processes affect more than one line of business?
	What opportunities are there to standardise processes and resources across LOBs?
	What data standards and principles should my project consider/align with?
	What information flows and structures require automation and transformation?
	What are the key activities in a business service or process?

EA Customer	Concerns and Questions
	Who are the custodians of Process, Data or Technology areas?
	Who are the Business Owner and/or SME for a particular application?
	What skills are available/needed to deliver the EA components of the future?
	What security concerns are applicable to the future EA components?
Human Resource/ Workforce Planners	What does the enterprise do?
	What does a particular line of business do and where do I fit in?
	What work is in progress and/or planned for a Division?
	How do I understand what other Divisions do?
	Where are the touch-points between mine and other division's activities?
Information Systems Security Managers	What are the information flow and transformation requirements of new activities?
	What information flow changes are associated with the business activities?
	What are the security classifications of new information flows?
Technology Implementers	Does my solution comply with IT direction?
	What technology components could my project could be re-using?
	What technology supports a particular business function?
	What technology delivers system functionality to a particular product/service?
	What business activities are being supported by a particular technology?
	What technical services do I need to support the system functions of a new app.?
	Is a particular IT application a good fit for my project requirements?
	What are the networks requirements of an information flow?
Business Process Improvement/Reeng ineering Analysts	What lines of business are not currently supported by technology?
	How much are my current business activities costing me?

EA Customer	Concerns and Questions
	Where are there potential opportunities for savings in business activities?
	Which areas of the business does my project impact/do we require support from?
Business Partners	What are the cross-organisation processes are we a part of?
	What are the business services we are to provide or consume?
	What information flows and data transformations support a business service?
	What business, data and technical standards apply to an information flow?
Franchisees/Branch Managers	What services can I provide?
	What activities and IT resources will I require for selected services?
	What information flows exist with head office?
Mergers and Acquisitions	What line of business activity gaps and overlaps exist between organisations?
	What technical service gaps and overlaps exist between organisations?
	What activities does the merged organisation perform that support our goals and initiatives?
	What merger investments overlap with our investments?
	Which investments do not align with our goals and initiatives?
Workforce	To what line of business do activities I perform belong?
	What performance measures are associated with my activities?
	Are my activities subject to changes to strategic or business drivers?
	What are the knowledge and skill requirements associated with my activities?

What are the types of EA products and services needed to meet EA customer objectives?

The type and make-up of the products and services an enterprise will provide are driven by their customers' needs and the objectives set for the customers, within the

Goals and Initiatives Layer, to convert strategic intent into tangible, changeable and implementable components.

In keeping with the concept of operations, vision and mission for the EA function, described in terms of a Use Case diagram, Figure 7 illustrates the types of services required of the EA function. The services are represented by use cases and the EA customers, or service consumers, as actors. A brief description for each of the services and the Customer perspective business objectives they seek to achieve are listed in Table 8 to help understand and explain what,and why, the services are are to be provided by the EA function.

In summary, the services break down into three main types:

1. Working with planners to arrive at an agreed, integrated target architecture and transition plan.
2. Engaging with resource planners and change agents to effect the transition plan and ensure progress towards the target architecture in a controlled way.
3. Providing the information captured about the current and target architectures, and the transition plan, in an accessible and useful manner to allow the various EA customers to plan, make decisions and/or perform their change activities in an informed manner.

Figure 7: EA Services (Artefact B-1)

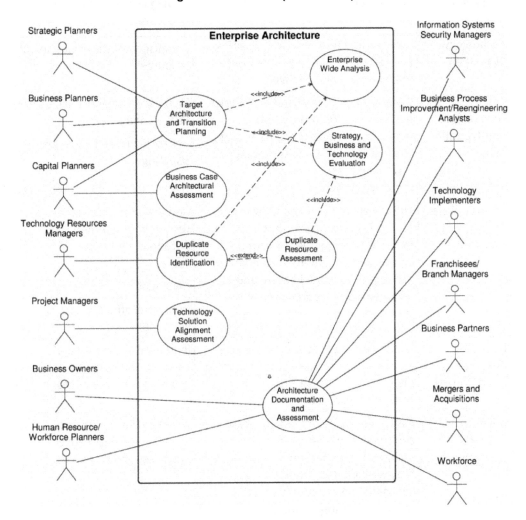

Table 8: EA Services to Customer Objectives (Management View)

EA Service	Description	Driving Customer Business Objective
Enterprise-wide Analysis	Documentation, assessment and/or design of components across an enterprise, or segment of the enterprise.	Increased integration from enterprise-wide planning and utilisation of resources
Strategy, Business and	The analysis of technology change requirements in lieu of strategic directions, business operations	Increased integration from enterprise wide planning and utilisation of resources

EA Service	Description	Driving Customer Business Objective
Technology Evaluation	changes and performance priorities and tactical technology or resource management perspective.	Increased holistic evaluation of resources
Target Architecture and Transition Planning	Development of a portfolio of work for business and/or information technology components, balancing strategy, business and technology drivers and associated future architecture.	Increased enterprise-wide and LOB planning decisions
		Improving effectiveness of planning
Business Case Architectural Assessment	The review of the technology solution sections of a business cases to ensure the investment is aligned with the agreed and documented standards and that future architecture and divergences are rationalised and reflected.	Reduced misunderstandings of resource requirements and potential solutions
		Increased holistic evaluation of resources
		Improving effectiveness of planning
Duplicate Resource Identification	Identification of the business and IT activities and resources that duplicate the function or service of another activity or resource.	Increased visualisation of valuable and duplicative processes and resources
Duplicate Resource Assessment	Assessment of identified duplicate components within the enterprise's architecture to determine whether they warrant decommissioning, consolidation or reuse within the context of strategic directions, business priorities and tactical requirements.	Increased visualisation of valuable and duplicative processes and resources
Architecture Documentation and Assessment	Publication of integrated strategy, business and technology current and/or future state information in a manner accessible and useful to an EA customer's activities.	Reduced time to gather and relate strategy, business and technology information
		Standardisation of information on processes and resources
		Reduced re-work on process and resource development within programs
		Reduced misunderstandings of resource requirements and potential solutions

Refer to the Appendix – Architecture Presentation Services Decomposition, for a breakdown of the principal types of architecture presentation services recommended for each of the key integrated governance functions and management processes.

What are the activities that the EA function must engage in to achieve the objectives of the EA as well as normal 'maintenance/housekeeping'?

Activities are the things the enterprise must perform to deliver its services, or core mission, and to act as a well-functioning and ongoing concern. The activities that it must excel at are those that directly contribute to achieving the Internal Process objectives from the Goals and Initiatives layer agreed on to address or leverage the influences internal to the enterprise.

Based on the earlier analysis in the Goals and Initiatives Layer, in summary the things that the EA function activities need to achieve are:

- Stakeholder and customer outcomes
- Building a valuable information asset for the enterprise
- Supporting the activities at which the EA function is required to excel.

The activities can therefore be divided into three main areas:

1. **The core mission activities of EA**. Generally speaking, these are the EA documentation method and management process activities that enable the delivery of the EA services.
2. **The establishment and ongoing management of the EA approach and supporting tools and repository**. The type of services being delivered by EA and the information required to support their delivery requires special data, analysis and presentation technologies and activities. These need to be identified and set up accordingly.
3. **The establishment and ongoing management of the EA program**.

Represented as a functional decomposition, illustrated in Figure 8 is the list of activities and sub-activities recommended for the EA function. The descriptions of the leaf-level activities are provided in Table 9. Following in Table 10 the leaf-level activities have been mapped against the Internal Process objectives to illustrate why they are needed and what they are to achieve if a fully functioning EA practice or capability is to be established.

Figure 8: EA Function Decomposition (Artefact B-4)

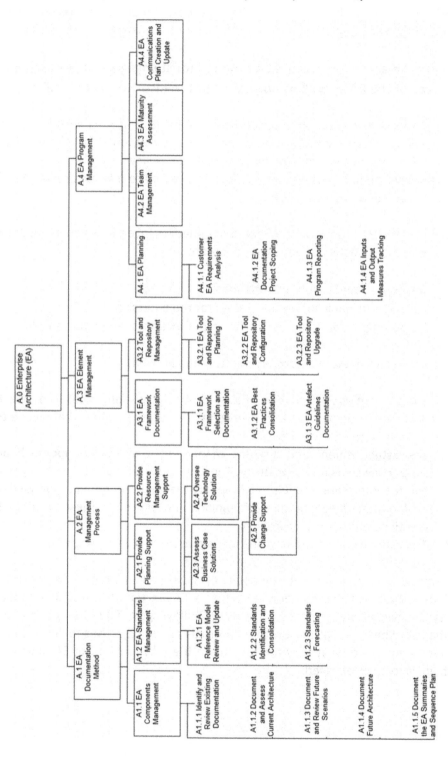

Table 9: EA Function Activity Definitions (Artefact B-4)

#	EA Activity	Description
1.1.1	Identify and Review Existing Documentation	Identification of current plans, summaries and views of EA components at each level of the framework and review for relevance or importance to the assessment and future state documentation. In many ways this activity is like taking an inventory of the components (strategic goals, business processes, measures, data, services, and IT resources) that already exist in the enterprise and mapping them to existing documentation.
1.1.2	Document and Assess Current Architecture	Involves the gathering, consolidation, massaging, linking and assessment against performance and asset management criteria of EA components currently in place to support the business.
1.1.3	Document and Review Future Scenarios	Involves assessing each key business objective and/or initiative, taking into account the strategic, business and technology drivers to identify the alternative operating scenarios relevant to the enterprise and agreeing on the ones to pursue within the planning horizon.
1.1.4	Document Future Architecture	Reflect approved scenarios and planning assumptions in and as the future architecture.
1.1.5	Document the EA Summaries and Sequence Plan	For general consumption and understanding, summarise the findings and the agreed scenarios and associated planning assumptions (gaps between scenario and current architecture) and identify the discrete investments that need to be made and the order and timeframe in which they can be reasonably executed.
1.2.1	EA Reference Model Review and Update	Involves assessing industry reference models for applicability and suitability and reflecting these as the enterprise's, or local, reference models.
1.2.2	Standards Identification and Consolidation	Gathering, setting and documenting the enterprise's protocols, specifications and products for the various local reference model definitions.
1.2.3	Standards Forecasting	Review and update of the local reference model trends, and determination of the relevance and impact of the trends on the enterprise architecture.
2.1	Provide Planning Support	Provide insights into the current architecture assessments, findings and emerging technologies, and the target architecture and transition plan into strategic, business and IT planning activities.
2.2	Provide Resource Management Support	Use of the local reference models, standards and forecast information to identify EA components that are candidates for reuse or decommissioning.

#	EA Activity	Description
2.3	Assess Business Case Solutions	Review and assess technology solution proposals (part of business cases work) for compliance with standards and the future architecture.
2.4	Oversee Technology Solution	Review, assess and guide technology development for compliance with standards and the future architecture.
2.5	Provide Change Support	Provision of information about the current and future state of the enterprise across all layers and threads and the plan to transition between the two.
3.1.1	EA Framework Selection and Documentation	Researching, selecting and introduction of an EA framework to the enterprise.
3.1.2	EA Best Practices Consolidation	Gathering, setting and documentation of the enterprises best practices relating to the modelling, planning and improvement of the enterprise from an S, B & T perspective.
3.1.3	EA Artefact Guidelines Documentation	Creation and update of Artefact Guidelines.
3.2.1	EA Tool and Repository Planning	This activity involves the tracking, evaluation and planning of changes to the software and hardware supporting the EA tool and repository.
3.2.2	EA Tool and Repository Configuration	This activity involves the configuration and customisation of the software, tools and repository that are necessary to help the management and presentation of the architecture data.
4.1.1	Customer EA Requirements Analysis	Review and discussion with other governance functions to determine their specific EA component documentation requirements, relationship requirements and view requirements.
4.1.2	EA Documentation Project Scoping	Identification of the scoping elements of the EA documentation project, such as segment, layers, EA components, purpose, and appetite for change.
4.1.3	EA Program Reporting	Production and update of standard reports about the progress and status of the EA program.
4.1.4	EA Inputs and Output Measures Tracking	Determines progress in the enablement of the core EA activities to establish and deliver value through the EA services.
4.2	EA Team Management	Roles and responsibilities assignment. Recruitment and training planning and execution.
4.3	EA Maturity Assessment	Measure and report on a multi- stage scale EA program implementation and use.

#	EA Activity	Description
4.4	EA Communications Plan Creation and Update	The development and update of the EA Communication Plan to articulate the EA documentation methodology and schedule of activities.

Table 10: EA Activities to Internal Process Objectives (Management View)

Grouping	Internal Process Objective	Key EA Activity
Customer Relationship	EA value scenario and questions understood and prioritised	Customer EA Requirements Analysis
	Customer satisfaction tracked	EA Communications Plan Creation and Update
		Customer EA Requirements Analysis
Innovation	EA best practices and relevant framework adopted	EA Framework Selection and Documentation
Operational Excellence - Documentation Method	Enterprise-wide architecture documented	Document and Assess Current Architecture
		Document Future Architecture
	Enterprise-wide architecture components classified	Document and Assess Current Architecture
		Document Future Architecture
	Architecture component standards integrated	Standards Identification and Consolidation
Operational Excellence - Management Process	Emerging trends researched and documented	Standards Forecasting
	EA Management Plans produced	Document and Review Future Scenarios
		Document the EA Summaries and Sequence Plan
	Technology assessment of all business cases	Assess Business Case Solutions

How does the EA function come together to deliver EA services?

Business activities independently don't deliver much value, but when arranged together or combined can contribute to the delivery of products or services of genuine value to customers.

The two key core mission areas of activity of the EA function are 1) the documentation method responsible for the documentation and assessment of the various current and future states as well as the EA Management plan; and 2) the management processes that will support the use of the documentation and EA Management plan by the various corporate and IT governance functions responsible for bringing about the changes that will deliver the target state.

The EA Element Management and EA Program Management are key underlying EA specific support activities required to plan, track and assure the ongoing success of the core mission EA function activities.

Described in terms of a value chain landscape diagram, illustrated in Figure 9, the EA function's activities are represented in a way to illustrate the sequential nature of the documentation method and management process activities, and the parallel and sequential nature of the supporting standards management documentation activities.

The supporting Element and Program Management activities are illustrated below the core mission activities to emphasis their supporting role, enabling the effective execution of the core mission activities.

Figure 9: EA Value Chain (Artefact B-4)

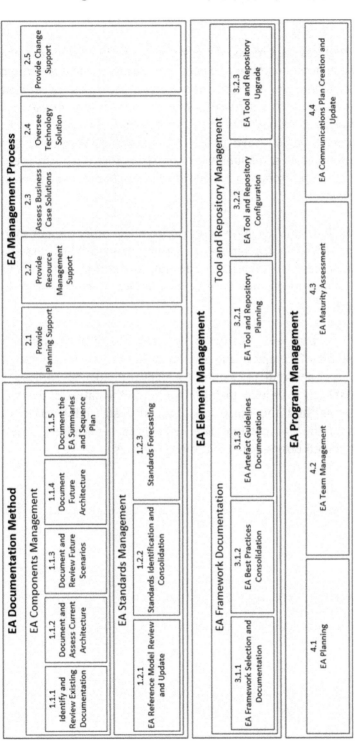

What business and/or enterprise services is the EA function likely to require?

Undertaking business, regardless of the industry, sector or services being delivered, requires support, access and use of a variety of business and enterprise services. For example, all organisations or organisational units regardless of product or service, whether they be a nation's defence organisation, a private or public hospital, HR business unit or strategy and planning function employ people, manage documents and store, update and retrieve data. These types of services that support the recruitment of employees, management and storage of documents, etc. can all be shared across the organisation to achieve efficiencies, improve consistency and reduce costs and complexity.

As such, the EA function, being no different from any other area of shared goal and activity, will need to call on a variety of common or shared business and enterprise services in the process of establishing, managing and performing EA activities. Where possible, the EA function should reuse existing or local standard enterprise processes or technologies.

Using the US Federal, and Australian derivative Service Reference Model as a representative list of common and shared business and enterprise services that organisations typically require, Figure 10 highlights specific services that the EA function is most likely to require, taking into account the nature of the documentation and data it uses, and the operational, security and information management requirements of the EA function. The highlighted services are described in the Appendix – Required Business and Enterprise Services.

Figure 10: EA Function Key Business and Enterprise Service Requirements (Management View)

Business Analytical Services

Analysis and Statistics	Business Intelligence
Forensics	Balanced Scorecard
Mathematical	Decision Support and Planning
Radiological	Demand Forecasting / Mgmt
Structural / Thermal	

Reporting	Knowledge Discovery
Ad hoc	Data Mining
OLAP	Modelling
Standardised / Canned	Simulation

Visualisation	
CAD	Graphing / Charting
Imagery	Mapping / Geospatial / Elevation / GPS
Multimedia	

Business Management Services

Supply Chain Management	Investment Management
Catalogue Management	Performance Management
Inventory Management	Portfolio Management
Invoice / Requisition Tracking and Approval	Strategic Planning and Mgmt
Logistics and Transportation	
Ordering / Purchasing	**Management of Process**
Procurement	Business Rule Management
Returns Management	Change Management
Sourcing Management	Configuration Management
Storefront / Shopping Cart	Governance / Policy Management
Warehouse Management	Program / Project Management
Organisational Management	Quality Management
Network Management	Requirements Management
Workgroup / Groupware	Risk Management

Process Automation Services

Tracking and Workflow	Routing and Scheduling
Case Management	Inbound Correspondence Management
Conflict Resolution	Outbound Correspondence Management
Process Tracking	

Back Office Services

Assets / Materials Management	Development and Integration
Asset Cataloguing / Identification	Data Integration
Asset Transfer, Allocation, and Maintenance	Enterprise Application Integration
Computers / Automation Management	Instrumentation and Testing
Facilities Management	Legacy Integration
Property / Asset Management	Software Development

Data Management	Human Capital / Workforce Management
Data Classification	
Data Cleansing	Contingent Workforce Management
Data Exchange	Resource Planning and Allocation
Data Mart	Skills Management
Data Recovery	Team / Org Management
Data Warehouse	Workforce Acquisition / Optimisation
Extraction and Transformation	Workforce Directory / Locator
Loading and Archiving	**Human Resources**
Meta Data Management	Awards Management
Financial Management	Benefit Management
Activity-Based Management	Career Development and Retention
Auditing	Education / Training
Billing and Accounting	Health and Safety
Credit / Charge	Personnel Administration
Currency Translation	Recruiting
Debt Collection	Resume Management
Expense Management	Retirement Management
Internal Controls	Time Reporting
Payment / Settlement	Travel Management
Payroll	
Revenue Management	

Customer Services

Customer Relationship Management	Customer Preferences
	Alerts and Notifications
Brand Management	Personalization
Call Centre Management	Subscriptions
Contact and Profile Management	**Customer-Initiated Assistance**
Customer / Account Management	Assistance Request
Customer Analytics	Multi-Lingual Support
Customer Feedback	Online Help
Partner Relationship Management	Online Tutorials
Product Management	Reservations / Registration
Sales and Marketing	Scheduling
Surveys	Self-Service

Legend

☐ Enterprise Services required by EA Activities

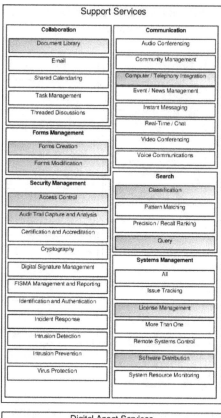

Refer to Appendix – Business and Enterprise Service Components by Dependent EA Activity, for the key EA activities identified as likely to need the highlighted services.

What should be considered when documenting and analysing the Products and Services Layer?

For an Enterprise

When documenting and analysing the Products and Services layer of the enterprise consider the following:

1. **Whose responsibility is it to architect a line of business within the enterprise in scope of the architecture?**

   The proposed EA function outlined in the reference architecture is primarily a CIO-sponsored function, supporting the CIO in his role as information officer to the organisation. In this capacity EA helps IT understand the information and communication technology (ICT) requirements from across the lines of business of the enterprise and to balance the competing strategic, business and technology drivers in order to come up with an ICT management plan that will best support the various lines of business change initiatives.

   Under this scenario, business analysis, that is, true business analysis, not the type that focuses on the business requirements of information systems, is the responsibility of the line of business manager and their delegates. That is, it's the business manager's responsibility to decide the required and/or achievable changes to his/her line of business architecture in response to the corporate and strategic plans and directions and their own internal process and performance issues and priorities. As business operations increasingly become dependent on ICT, these plans are invariably and necessarily covering components in the lower layers of the architecture as well.

   For EA to provide value to those responsible for planning the Products and Services layer, in increasing level of contribution and value, EAs should consider:

   o Providing the standards and guidelines for documenting business changes that will aid the consistency in representation and communications of planning decisions, and describe impacts in terms accessible and usable across the line of business and by various change agents.
   o Performing specific analysis around particular processes or resources that are important to a line of business to help aid its business

planning process. For example, identifying opportunities for application rationalisation or 'piggy-backing' on changes planned elsewhere in the organisation.

o   Reviewing line of business plans against the EA Management Plan for alignment with cross-enterprise initiatives, opportunities and conflicts.

o   Performing the analysis of the strategic plan and assessment of the Products and Services layer components on behalf of line of business managers for input to their plans.

2. **Lines of business plans provide input to the Goals and Initiatives, and Products and Services layers.**

One of the primary aims of the business plan is to answer the questions of what core mission and intra-enterprise and business services need to be delivered, managed and implemented, and to some extent, how this should occur. Each line of business plan, however, contains not only these details but also the goals the line of business has set itself to demonstrate that change is being achieved, and the initiatives planned to be undertaken to bring about these changes.

Some of these objectives and initiatives focus on the contribution to the line of business' shareholders good, some to the external and internal customers of their line of business, some specific to their internal processes, and finally, others are to do with enablement of their people and information. In summary, the same type of information documented in the Goals and Initiatives layer, and in particular, the information represented in the Balanced Scorecard. Therefore, information from lines of business plans and corporate, or strategic, plans contribute to documenting the Goals and Initiatives layer.

Following the approach that has been used in the Goals and Initiative layer to document an enterprise's goals, to identify and/or document the objectives and initiatives within line of business plans, will help balance and explain the line of business' planned goals and initiatives.

From a documentation perspective, line of business goals and initiatives can either be aggregated into a single enterprise Balanced Scorecard or into separate Balanced Scorecards for each line of business. Common or shared objectives and initiatives can be present in each to illustrate contribution from, or to, the scorecards to other lines of business.

3. **Don't labour on the shared enterprise and business services.**

The focus of documentation and analysis within the Products and Services layer should be the core mission products and services of the enterprise being architected. While shared business and enterprise services will play an important part in building and supporting the capabilities to deliver the enterprise's products and services, it is best to consider what it means to be the customer of these services and how they are, or are not, able to support the enterprise's capabilities.

For example, for the purposes of the reference architecture the EA function is treated as the enterprise, although it is a delivery support business service by definition. While it, in turn, relies on various other business and enterprise services to deliver its EA services, it is not necessary to treat each to the same detailed analysis. First, it would create a lot of effort, and second it would not contribute greatly to understanding or planning the EA function. Knowing whether a business or enterprise service exists, however, is important, and how and when it will be delivered to ensure the core mission services of the enterprise are able to be delivered efficiently will become a key dependency, or part of the transition plan.

4. **To Process Map or Not.**

As with all models, different audiences require slightly different perspectives relevant to their decision-making responsibilities.

The key thing about Process Maps that make them most effective is their ability to answer multiple questions. In particular, why are we doing this, who or what is responsible for doing things, when does it get done and what information is needed to do it? Specifically, they answer the question 'how do we do what we need to do'.

Detailed process mapping is an effective method of drawing out and illustrating current manual and automated tasks performed to deliver a service or function within an organisation, and the actual method by which a service or function is or will be performed. This level of detail is essential for process improvement and simulation exercises, and for training and induction purposes.

Detailed process mapping, however, is time consuming, and results in a significant amount of data when done for even a small number of lines of business. If a process mapping exercise is not supported by a suitable documentation and repository methodology, the management of the data and the use of the data for any purpose other than as a visual representation of 'how we do things' can be greatly limited.

Function modelling, at the other end of the process spectrum, focuses on what the organisation 'needs to be able to do' rather than how it does it. There is generally only one functional model for the enterprise, and it is enterprise-wide. As such, it is capable of representing at a high level the current or future requirements of the capabilities of the organisation. The model in Figure 8 is an example of a Function model representing what the proposed EA function 'needs to be able to do'.

In between process maps and functional models are various types and levels of process models. For example:

- o Activity flow models (based on the IDEF0 notation), which focus on answering the question 'what information is needed to do a function', but not 'who or when'. Activity flows can be decomposed to show how sub-functions/activities in turn consume and provide information, see Appendix – The Activity Information Flow Decomposition for examples relevant to the EA function. At the highest level is a context view focusing on the information consumed and provided external to the enterprise. Figure 11 in the Data and Information layer section is a context level Activity flow model to represent the information requirements of the EA function.
- o Analysis level process maps drop much of the detail of the detailed process maps, such as gateways, events and information inputs and outputs, and summarise or group detailed processes together, to answer questions such as 'who is responsible for what types of activities' and at a high level, 'when'.
- o Sequence or event diagrams. These focus on answering 'who', and at a high level, 'when and what information flow in and out of the components', but drop the 'what is being done'. These were used to help illustrate the potentially different timings for the production of the EA Management Plan depending on whether it's meant to provide input to Business Plans, or to use Business Plans as inputs.

In summary, use the following as a guide as to when to include and perform each of the business model types:

- o A function model for most EA customer service scenarios where it is important to communicate what the enterprise currently does today, and what they need to include in the target. Also to support the highlighting, contextualising and description of the capability changes associated with specific functions.

- o Activity Flow model documentation and analysis when information requirements across a large number of activities within the enterprise or segment are important.
- o Analysis level process map documentation and assessment when assigning functional responsibilities across business units, functional areas, externals, etc. for significant service delivery or implementation processes.
- o Detailed process map documentation and analysis when the governance function that EA is integrating with is performing process improvement, and it is important to show the current and target state of a process and what needs to be done to move between the two. This should focus and be limited to a few specific or high priority enterprise-wide processes or lines of business. For example, as part of a project or solution architecture. Avoid trying to detail process map for other EA customer types.
- o Sequence or event documentation and analysis when the sequence and timing of information flows between key components is of most importance.

For the EA function

When using the reference architecture to document and analyse the EA function's Products and Services layer:

1. **Plan the EA services to deliver**

   The types of EA services identified in the reference architecture cover the full spectrum of governance and management customers, and documentation and analysis, necessary to meet all objectives outlined in the previous section. The types of EA services to be delivered initially will significantly vary the types of EA function processes and resources that are required. While the results of the Goals and Initiatives documentation and analysis will point to some types of EA services being more attractive than others, some of these attractive EA services may not be immediately achievable. Use Section 9 - The EA Program and Transition Plan, to help decide and plan the rollout plan of EA services.

2. **Assess the current EA function's capabilities**

   Score the activities in the Documentation Method and Management Process activity areas of the reference architecture to baseline the EA function's current capability to deliver EA services.

Score the activities within the EA Element and EA Program Management activity areas to baseline the EA function's current capability to operate and extend the EA capability.

A good approach to scoring the EA function is to use a capability maturity model approach. For example, use zero to denote 'not performed, or have just started', through to 5 for 'continuously improving' based on data gathered about the performance of the activity.

Whatever scoring method is adopted, to help highlight areas of required establishment and enhancement, it is important that the reason, or rationale, for the scores is well documented and that they clearly:

- o Refer to the layer and/or thread component within the architecture that is being scored
- o Describe in terms of their existence and/or ability, and/or capacity, to be performed
- o Identify the existence and/or ability, and/or capacity, of any business, enterprise or technical service on which they depend.

3. **Highlight the EA function's Products and Services components**

Using the diagrams and definitions provided in the reference architecture as a basis, highlight the components in the Products and Services layer that will ultimately make up the EA function, and the timeframes when they are planned to be operational.

4. **Update the business objectives in the Internal Process perspective**

Update the business objectives in the Goals and Initiatives Layer, in particular the Internal Process perspective of the Balanced Scorecard, setting the performance measures to reflect the improvements and changes to the services and activities of the EA function that are being sought.

Example CMM based targets:

- Achieve CMM level 3, that is, well defined, standard processes and organisational learning, in EA Communications Plan Creation and Update, within 6 months
- Achieve CMM level 2, that is, planned and tracked, in Standards Forecasting, within 12 months.

5. **Identify existing capabilities capable of delivering business and enterprise services requirements**

The EA function must practice what it preaches, and where possible try and reuse the business and enterprise services available within the organisation. This will allow it to leverage and benefit from these services' best practices, standards and workforce (their EA threads) to support and/or realise the delivery of the EA function's services, and to optimise the performance of the EA activities.

If a business and enterprise service reference model is not already employed within the organisation, use the one provided in the reference architecture, otherwise use the one in use by the enterprise to help identify, classify and assess the services and threads that the EA function must, or may, use.

If the presence or capacity of the available services is not suitable to the EA function's needs, include in the plan the methods to fulfil or realise these appropriate to its needs. This may involve:

- o Delivering the EA function service or performing the EA function with no input from the enterprise
- o Delivering the EA function service or performing the EA function with no external support, but according to the enterprise's best practices and standards
- o Helping the enterprise to identify and prioritise additional capacity requirements
- o Helping the enterprise to establish and resource as part of its EA management plan and consuming the resultant services;
- o A combination of the above.

Section 3 – The Data and Information of the EA function

Once the business services and activities have been identified, it is important to ask the following of the enterprise:

- What are the flows of information that will be required within and between activities in order to make them successful?
- How will the data underlying the information flows be formatted, generated, shared, and stored?
- How will the data become useable information and knowledge?

Having the Data and Information layer as the next layer of the architecture enforces the notion of the type of enterprise architecture being espoused and performed. In this case, one aimed at planning and overseeing information and communications technology in support of business operations. This is in contrast to system architecture, for example, whose frameworks are focused on the manufacture and support for the delivery of mostly non information-related products and services, such as factories for the manufacturing of goods, equipment and materials for the development of aircraft, and networks to provide commercial telecommunications services.

In enterprises whose products and services are mostly non information-related, enterprise architecture focuses on the information and communications to support the operational aspects of delivering the products and services, but is not so concerned about the processes and resources that produce the organisation's products and services. In a knowledge-centric enterprise, however, EA plays a far more important role in the delivery of the enterprise's products and services, and the data and information layer will include the information-based products and services of the enterprise as well as the supporting information and communications that support the operational aspects of the enterprise.

As an EA function is a governance function and management process, and as such principally a knowledge-centric enterprise, its products and services are largely knowledge and information-based, and therefore its information requirements cover both its EA services and the operations of the EA function.

What EA documentation and data is required to meet EA customer information requirements?

One of the key drivers and core services of the EA function is helping other governance functions and management processes to make better decisions through the provision of information, and using the results of analysis on the current and future states, for the enterprise to plan to bring about the change. That is, providing the integrated architectural perspectives and analysis that is consistent with the EA vision and mission.

In Table 11, each of the various EA customer questions are listed and against each are described the types of architectural view or assessment that the EA function should aim to provide to improve decision-making, and the key types enterprise component that are key or core to the view and assessment.

The terms EA component and enterprise component are interchangeable and include all types of objects, at each layer of the architecture, that the EA function intends to document and analyse.

Table 11: EA View and Assessments by EA Customer Question

EA Customer	Question	View/Assessment Description	Key Components
Capital Planners	What opportunities are there to consolidate process and resources across LOBs?	Systems functions that provide select service components.	Systems Functions
			Service Components
	How is the business and IT spend aligned to the strategic direction of the organisation?	Investments and the strategic initiatives that they implement.	Investments
			Strategic Initiatives
		Investments that are not linked to any strategic initiatives.	Investments
			Strategic Initiatives
	Where are there potential overlaps in scope between projects/programs of work?	Enterprise components associated with two or more investments to assist identification of overlaps.	Investments
			EA Components
			Change Requests

EA Customer	Question	View/Assessment Description	Key Components
	Does a project take into account all the business functions that it should?	Future and/or changed activities associated with the investment or strategic initiative that the investment implements.	Investments
			Activities
			Strategic Initiatives
	Where are we focusing our investments (active and proposed) and how does it relate to expected returns?	Future and/or changed activities associated with the select investments or strategic initiatives that the investments implement.	Investments
			Activities
			Strategic Initiatives
		Enterprise components, i.e., processes and resources, associated with the select investments or strategic initiatives that the investments implement.	Investments
			EA Components
			Strategic Initiatives
	How are our investments aligned to our corporate strategic direction?	Investments and the strategic initiatives that they implement.	Investments
			Strategic Initiatives
		Investments that are not linked to any strategic initiatives.	Investments
			Strategic Initiatives
	What are our priorities for focusing investments and effort?	Objectives and influences associated with select investments.	Business Objectives
			Investments
			EA Components
		Activities in other lobs with which the select investment activities exchange data.	Investments
			Activities
			Information Flows
Strategic Planners	How is the business and IT spend aligned to the	Investments and the strategic initiatives that they implement.	Investments
			Strategic Initiatives

EA Customer	Question	View/Assessment Description	Key Components
	strategic direction of the organisation?	Investments that are not linked to any strategic initiatives.	Investments
			Strategic Initiatives
			IT Principles
		New or changed information flows in the future architecture and the deltas/gaps to the current information flows.	Information Flows
	How are the business capabilities of the enterprise positioned to support delivery of the corporate strategic direction?	Strategic initiatives and the current capabilities to support their implementation or delivery.	Strategic Initiatives
			Capabilities
	Where are we focusing our investments (active and proposed) and how does it relate to expected returns?	Future and/or changed activities associated with the select investments or strategic initiatives that the investments implement.	Investments
			Activities
			Strategic Initiatives
		Enterprise components, i.e., processes and resources, associated with the select investments or strategic initiatives that the investments implement.	Investments
			EA Components
			Strategic Initiatives
	How are our investments aligned to our corporate strategic direction?	Investments and the strategic initiatives that they implement.	Investments
			Strategic Initiatives
		Investments that are not linked to any strategic initiatives.	Investments
			Strategic Initiatives
	What components of our business are	Relationships from strategy components	EA Components
			Business Objectives

EA Customer	Question	View/Assessment Description	Key Components
	required to support a specific marketplace opportunity?	to activities and technology components.	Strategic Initiatives
		Required and used technology services and components respectively for select activities.	Technology
			Activities
			Applications
			Technical Reference Model
	How can I assess what the enterprise can leverage to exploit potential emerging market opportunities?	Activities required to perform and support the select business services.	Activities
			Business Services
	What pipeline activity would support a particular new product or market?	Activity changes planned as part of the strategic initiatives and investments where the status is still not implemented.	Investments
			Activities
			Requirements
	What internal business services could be leveraged to provide an external customer offering?	Business and enterprise services, and their current state, and the current business functions and core mission services they support.	Business Services
			Activities
	What opportunities/ alternative models, e.g. consolidation, outsourcing vs. in-sourcing, exist for delivering services in the enterprise?	Solution options analysis associated with the select business services.	Business Services
			Solution Options Analysis
	How can I compare/benchmark the enterprise's performance and spending with other	Performance measures of objectives directly or indirectly related to select activities.	Activities
			Business Objectives
			Performance Measures

EA Customer	Question	View/Assessment Description	Key Components
	organisations/other industry competitors?		
	What does it cost to deliver a particular business function?	Activities associated with select functions, the people and technology associated with the performance of the activities, and the annualised costs proportioned across the activities.	Activities
			Activities Cost Analysis
	What are the current 'pain points' for my Line of Business?	Influences associated with the activities of select lines of business.	Activities
			Influences
	What are the impacts across different Lines of Business if a new market or product/service offering is pursued/ introduced?	Activities and resources that support select business services and/or products.	EA Components
			Business Services
	How do we come together as an organisation to deliver products and services to customers (from an end-to-end value chain perspective)?	Value chain of the core activities of the enterprise or select segments.	Business Services
	What are our priorities for focusing investments and effort?	Objectives and influences associated with select investments.	Business Objectives
Business Planner	What business activities in my line of business are required or affected to support strategic direction and business performance priorities?	Relationships between select strategy components and business activities.	Activities
			Business Objectives
			Strategic Initiatives
	What are the strategic drivers and directions of	Strengths, weaknesses,	Strategic Initiatives
			Influences

EA Customer	Question	View/Assessment Description	Key Components
	the enterprise/segment?	opportunities and threats, and associated strategic and business plans for the enterprise or select segment.	
	What are the future required or affected business activities identified to support the strategic drivers and directions?	Activities strategically important or with priority business performance issues.	Activities
			Business Objectives
			Influences
		Future and/or changed activities associated with select investments or strategic initiatives that the investments implement.	Investments
			Activities
			Strategic Initiatives
	What is the current transition plan for my line of business?	Investments and impacted components where the investments or impacted components are owned by the line of business.	Organisational Units
			Investments
			EA Components
	What future required or affected business activities within this line of business still remain unimplemented?	Activity changes planned as part of the strategic initiatives and investments where the status is still not implemented.	Investments Activities Requirements
	What performance issues are associated with business activities within this line of business?	Activities that do not use applications or that have information flows that do not have system exchanges associated with them, and where an assessment has identified performance issues.	Activities
			Information Flows
			Performance Assessment
			Activities

EA Customer	Question	View/Assessment Description	Key Components
	What current business activities are duplicated across this and other lines of business?	Activities performed by the select organisational unit(s).	Organisational Units
	What information flow and data transformations does the current knowledge plan support?	Standards associated with select activities that provide or consume the exchange, the entities and attributes contained in the flow and the technologies (if applicable) that automate the exchange.	Information Flows
			System Reference Architecture
			IT Principles
Business Owners	What is the current transition plan/ investments for my line of business?	Future and/or changed activities associated with the investment or strategic initiative that the investment implements.	Investments
			Activities
			Strategic Initiatives
	What business activities in my line of business are required or affected to support strategic direction and business performance priorities?	Relationship between select strategy components and business activities.	Activities
			Business Objectives
			Strategic Initiatives
	What performance and output measures are associated with the business activities requirements and changes?	Performance measures of the objectives directly or indirectly related to a set of activities.	Activities
			Business Objectives
			Performance Measures
	What are the information flow and data transformation requirements of new business activities?	New or changed information flows in the future architecture and the deltas/gaps to the current information flows.	Information Flows

EA Customer	Question	View/Assessment Description	Key Components
	What produces or consumes the information flows of required business activities?	Information flows with a select set of activities and the activities at the other end of the exchanges and owning line of business.	Activities
			Information Flows
	What are the information flow and transformation automation changes associated with the required and affected business activities?	New or changed information flows in the future architecture and the deltas/gaps to the current information flows.	Information Flows
	How effective have executed investments been?	Performance metrics applicable to the investment and an assessment of progress against target.	Investments
			Performance Measure Status
Technology Resource Managers	Where is there opportunity for replacing or decommissioning IT systems?	Service components and technical services and their implementing enterprise components.	EA Components
			Data Reference Model
			Service Reference Model
			Technical Reference Model
	Which LOBs rely on a large number of applications (and interfaces) to perform their operations?	Activities with the greatest number of automations.	Activities
			Information Flows
			System Data Exchanges
	Where are there potential overlaps in application capability/ system functionality (e.g. presentation, capture, transformation, calculation)?	System functions implemented by one of more applications.	Systems Functions
			Applications

EA Customer	Question	View/Assessment Description	Key Components
	What business functions are impacted by a decision to invest in a specific technology?	Required and used technology services and components respectively for activities of interest.	Technology
			Activities
			Applications
			Technical Reference Model
	What are the knowledge and skill areas for a particular technology/application?	Knowledge and skill areas for the select technology components.	Technology
			Knowledge and Skills
	What business functions are being supported by a particular technology/IT Application?	Required and used technology services and components respectively for select activities.	Technology
			Activities
			Applications
			Technical Reference Model
Project Manager	How is my investment aligned to our corporate strategic direction?	Investments and the strategic initiatives that they implement.	Investments
			Strategic Initiatives
		Investments that are not linked to any strategic initiatives.	Investments
			Strategic Initiatives
	Where are there potential overlaps in scope between projects/programs of work?	Enterprise components associated with two or more investments to assist identification of overlaps.	Investments
			EA Components
			Change Requests
	Does a project take into account all the business functions that it should?	Future and/or changed activities associated with the investment or strategic initiative that the investment implements.	Investments
			Activities
			Strategic Initiatives
	What are the cross-divisional considerations and dependencies (if any) for this project?	Activities in other lobs with which the investment activities exchange data.	Investments
			Activities
			Information Flows

EA Customer	Question	View/Assessment Description	Key Components
	What are the lines of business activities and processes within my identified scope?	Future and/or changed activities associated with the investment or strategic initiative that the investment implements.	Investments
			Activities
			Strategic Initiatives
	What should my project be including in its scope?	Relationships from select strategy components to business activities and technology components.	EA Components
			Business Objectives
			Strategic Initiatives
	What are the active or planned programs of work that effect/will affect the same functions my project will?	Future and/or changed activities associated with the investment or strategic initiative that the investment implements.	Investments
			Activities
			Strategic Initiatives
	How do I understand and reflect the impact of a change request for the scope of my project?	Enterprise components associated with two or more investments to assist identification of overlaps.	Investments
			EA Components
			Change Requests
	What are the future EA components to be delivered and changed by this project?	Enterprise components, i.e., processes and resources, associated with select investments or strategic initiatives the investments implement.	Investments
			EA Components
			Strategic Initiatives
	What business services or processes affect more than one line of business?	The activities performed by the organisational unit(s) of interest.	Activities
			Organisational Units
			Activities

EA Customer	Question	View/Assessment Description	Key Components
	What opportunities are there to standardise or consolidate processes, functions and technology across lines of business?	Activities performed by the organisational unit(s) of interest.	Organisational Units
	With what data standards and principles should my project consider/align?	Security principles associated to the future ea components selected.	EA Components
			Security Principles
		Data and information standards associated with select data components within the future architecture.	Entity
			Information Flows
			Data and Information Standard
	What information flows and structures (addresses, products, customers, etc.) should my application automate?	Activities that do not use applications or that have information flows that do not have system exchanges associated with them and where an assessment has identified performance issues.	Activities
			Information Flows
			Performance Assessment
	What are the key activities in a business service or process?	Activities required to perform and support the business service.	Activities
			Business Services
	Who are the custodians of key Process, Data or Technology areas (e.g. Customer subject area)?	Enterprise components and the organisational units with a custodial relationship.	EA Components
			Organisational Units
	Who are the Business Owner and/or SME for a particular application?	Enterprise components and the organisational units with an owner relationship.	EA Components
			Organisational Units
			EA Components

EA Customer	Question	View/Assessment Description	Key Components
	What skills are available/needed to be supplemented to deliver the required or affected EA components of the future architecture?	Knowledge and skills areas for select enterprise components.	Knowledge and Skills
	What security considerations need to be considered for EA components within the future architecture?	Security principles associated to select future enterprise components.	EA Components
			Security Principles
Human Resource/ Workforce Planners	What does the enterprise do and how does it work together to deliver its value proposition/s in the marketplace?	Activities performed by select organisational units.	Activities
			Organisational Units
	What does a particular Division do and where do I fit in?	Activities performed by select organisational units.	Activities
			Organisational Units
	What work is in progress and/or planned for a Division?	Investments and the strategic initiatives that they implement.	Investments
			Strategic Initiatives
	How do I understand what other Divisions do and/or where the touch-points are with my Division/set of activities?	Activities performed by select organisational units.	Activities
			Organisational Units
	How do I understand what other Divisions do and/or where the touch-points are with my Division/set of activities?	Information flows for select activities and the activities at the other end of the exchanges, and their owning line of business.	Activities
			Information Flows
Information Systems	What are the information flow and data transformation	New or changed information flows in the future architecture	Information Flows

EA Customer	Question	View/Assessment Description	Key Components
Security Manager	requirements of new business activities?	and the deltas/gaps to the current information flows.	
	What are information flow and transformation automation changes associated with the required and affected business activities?	New or changed information flows in the future architecture and the deltas/gaps to the current information flows.	Information Flows
	What are the security classifications of new and changed information flows within the future architecture?	New or changed information flows in the future architecture and the deltas/gaps to the current information flows.	Information Flows
Technology Implementer	Does my solution comply with IT direction?	Assessment of a proposed implementation against the standards and future architecture.	Investments
			EA Components
	What are the appropriate technology components that my project could be re-using?	Service components and technical services and their implementing ea components.	EA Components
			Data Reference Model
			Service Reference Model
			Technical Reference Model
	What technology supports a particular business function?	Activities and resources that support select business services and/or products.	EA Components
			Business Services
	What technology delivers system functionality to support a particular or new product or service?	Activities and resources that support select business services and/or products.	EA Components
			Business Services
			Technology

EA Customer	Question	View/Assessment Description	Key Components
	What business functions are being supported by a particular technology/IT Application?	Required and used technology services and components respectively for select activities.	Activities
			Applications
			Technical Reference Model
	What technical services do I need to support the business services to be delivered by a new application?	Select current or future system functions mapped against the technical services required to implement them.	Systems Functions
			Technical Reference Model
	Is a particular IT application a good fit for my project requirements?	Required investment system functions versus those of the select applications.	Investments
			Systems Functions
			Applications
		Technology standards profile mapped to select applications for fit.	Applications
			Technology
			Technical Reference Model
	What information flows with head office exist?	Information flows associated with the select operational nodes and/or systems nodes.	Information Flows
Business Process Improvement/ Reengineering Analyst	What lines of business are not currently supported by technology capability?	Activities that do not use applications or that have information flows that do not have system exchanges associated with them and where an assessment has identified performance issues with this.	Activities
			Information Flows
			Performance Assessment
	How much are my current business processes/ activities costing me, and where	People and technology associated with the performance of the select activities, and	Activities

EA Customer	Question	View/Assessment Description	Key Components
	are there potential opportunities for savings?	the annualised costs proportioned across the activities.	
	How much are my current business processes/ activities costing me, and where are there potential opportunities for savings?	Service components and technical services and their implementing enterprise components.	EA Components
			Data Reference Model
			Service Reference Model
			Technical Reference Model
	Which area/s of the business does my project impact or require support from for delivery?	Future and/or changed activities associated with the select investments or strategic initiative that the investments implement.	Investments
			Activities
			Strategic Initiatives
		Enterprise components, i.e., processes and resources, associated with select investments or strategic initiatives the investments implement.	Investments
			EA Components
			Strategic Initiatives
Business Partners	What are the cross-organisation processes to be achieved?	Activities required to be performed and that support the delivery of select business services.	Business Services
			Activities
	What are the business services to be provided/ consumed?	Future and/or changed activities associated with the select investments or strategic initiative that the investments implement.	Investments
			Activities
			Strategic Initiatives
			Activities

EA Customer	Question	View/Assessment Description	Key Components
	What are the information flows and data transformations supporting the business services?	Information flows used and provided by select services and supporting activities.	Information Flows
			Business Services
	What business, data and technical standards are to be implemented for the information flows?	Standards associated with the activities that provide or consume the exchange, the entities and attributes contained in the flow and the technologies (if applicable) that automate the exchange.	Information Flows
			System Reference Architecture
			IT Principles
Franchisees/ Branch Managers	What services can I provide?	Services for select lines of business.	Business Services
	What activities and IT resources will I require for selected services?	Activities and resources that support select business services and/or products.	EA Components
			Business Services
	What information flows with head office exist?	Information flows associated with the select operational nodes and/or systems nodes.	Information Flows
			Needlines
Mergers and Acquisitions	What line of business activity gaps and overlaps exist between our and their organisation?	Activities performed by select organisational units.	Activities
			Organisational Units
	What technical services gaps and overlaps exist between our and their organisation?	Service components and technical services and their implementing enterprise components.	EA Components
			Data Reference Model
			Service Reference Model
			Technical Reference Model

EA Customer	Question	View/Assessment Description	Key Components
	What activities does the potential acquisition perform that support our goals and initiatives?	Capabilities of the enterprise, those that a merger or acquisition has, and the strategic initiatives associated with those capabilities.	Strategic Initiatives
			Capabilities
	What merger investments overlap with our investments?	Enterprise components associated with two or more investments to assist identify overlaps.	Investments
			EA Components
			Change Requests
	Which investments do not align with our goals and initiatives?	Investments that are not linked to any strategic initiatives.	Investments
			Strategic Initiatives
Workforce	To what line of business does the business service and activities I perform belong?	Activities performed by select organisational units.	Activities
			Organisational Units
	What are the performance outcomes and output measures associated with my business service and activities?	Performance measures of the objectives directly or indirectly related to a select set of activities.	Activities
			Business Objectives
			Performance Measures
	Are the business service and activities I perform subject to changes to strategic direction or business priorities?	Relationships from select strategy components to business activities and technology components.	EA Components
			Business Objectives
			Strategic Initiatives
		Activities strategically important or with priority business performance issues.	Activities
			Business Objectives
			Influences
	What are the knowledge and skill requirements associated with my	Knowledge and skill areas required or people doing select activities.	Activities
			Knowledge and Skills

EA Customer	Question	View/Assessment Description	Key Components
	business service and activities?		

What types of information flows are required to support the EA function's service delivery and operational responsibilities?

While the core activities of the Enterprise Architecture function are the management and provision of EA information in support of its customers, other information also needs to be consumed and provided to support and enable these core activities. Described using an activity flow or IDEF0 diagram, in Figure 11 are illustrated the main EA information flows and the chief external entities with which an EA function typically provides and consumes information during the course of delivering and operating the EA services and function. In the Appendix – Principal EA Information Flow Descriptions, descriptions of each of the information flows in Figure 11 are provided.

Figure 11: A-0 EA Function activity flows (Artefact D-2)

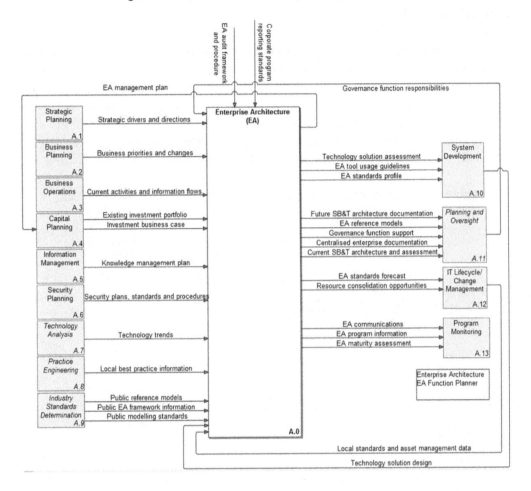

In the Products and Services layer a decomposition of the EA function into activities was provided. These activities are responsible for using and producing the information flows above. Described in terms of the IDEF0 Activity Flow notation, in the Appendix – The Activity Information Flow, the activities responsibilities are illustrated.

Where in the organisation do the providers and consumers of EA information reside?

A variety of information is consumed and provided by an EA function, as illustrated above, in order for it to deliver a quality service and to operate effectively. Described in terms of an Operational Node Connectivity diagram, where by an Operational Node is a geographical, organisational or functional area where activities take place. Figure 12 summarises the information needs of the EA function to help illuminate the key lines of communication and information sharing that need to be organised, facilitated and made efficient to maximise EA service delivery and operations.

Figure 12: Indicative Integrated Governance Information Needs (Artefact B-2)

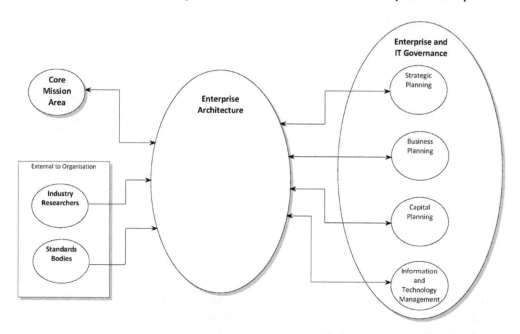

What are the key sequences of information flow with the EA function?

One of the most significant timing considerations of the EA function is the timing of the development of the EA Management Plan. Described in terms of a sequence diagram, Figure 13 illustrates the traditional sequencing of activities for the EA function aimed at IT investment portfolio determination. The key message here is that EA management planning occurs following strategic planning and business planning within the lines of business in scope of the EA. At this point, much of the business architecture details have been finalised leading the EA function to focus on documenting the EA to optimise the planning of the IT architecture.

Figure 13: EA Target Architecture and Transition Planning Event Trace - IT focused (Artefact D-4)

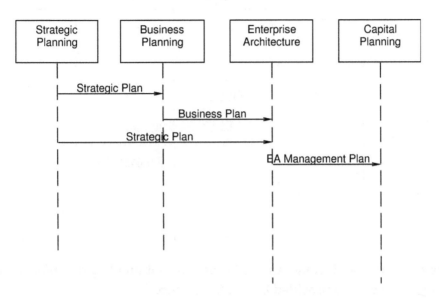

Enterprise architecture, however, also has the potential to support business planning activities, and is used by certain organisations in this manner. Within the US Department of Defense, EA is already used to support what it refers to as its Functional Area Analysis. Under this scenario, EA management planning precedes the Business Planning activity. Described in terms of a sequence diagram, illustrated in Figure 14 is EA management planning undertaken immediately after strategic planning. This in no way means that Business Planners are replaced by Enterprise Architects. During the EA management planning activity Business Planners will be one of the principal contributors to the business layer analysis and design, and for all intents and purposes they are the acting business architects and a part of the EA team. Their efforts, however, in line with EA principles, will be employed and guided to take an enterprise-wide and strategic, business and technology-driven perspective.

Figure 14: EA Target Architecture and Transition Planning Event Trace - Business and IT focused (Artefact D-4)

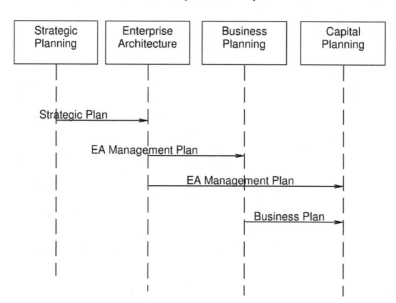

What key data and documentation items are contained by the information flows consumed and provided by the EA function?

All enterprises provide and consume data and documentation with their customers and service providers. Sometimes these may even make up the core products and services of the enterprise, as is the case for the EA function. Understanding what data and documentation is available or is required to be provided to the enterprise, and that is capable or necessary to be provided by the enterprise is critical for understanding the gap between the enterprises data requirements and what is currently available. This is particularly important for understanding the type of data analysis, transformation, management, presentation, etc. that will be required to support or perform the delivery of the enterprise's services.

Identifying and describing the content of the information flows according to a single and consistent data and documentation glossary helps achieve consensus and understanding across the enterprise regarding specific and overlapping data and information usage and requirements as well as the movement and transformation of data and information throughout the enterprise.

For the EA function, the most important output information flows are those that will provide the views and assessments listed against the EA questions in this layer, and that help to answer EA customer questions in support of their decision-making activities. These views and assessments form part of, and provide detailed specifications for, the principal documentation outputs of the EA function, i.e., the Current Architecture Assessment, Future Architecture and EA Management Plan.

The input information flows can be broken into two types: 1) plans and artefacts that directly contribute to the EA core mission activities, for example, strategic plans, business plans, security plans, knowledge or information management plans, and 2) information that help guide and govern the EA function, for example:

- The knowledge of the outputs and requirements of other business and IT governance functions and management processes
- The available standards, reference models, etc. available to support business and IT governance
- Information about current business and IT trends

In Table 12 are listed the principal information flows consumed and provided by the EA function decomposed to the key types of component data and documentation they can be expected or are required to comprise of, and provide. For descriptions of the documentation and data items listed below, refer to the Appendix – The EA Data Dictionary and Glossary.

Table 12: EA Function Information Flows Documentation and Data (Artefact D-2)

Information Flow	Data and/or Documentation	Data and/or Documentation	Data and/or Documentation	Data and/or Documentation
Business priorities and changes	Business Plan	Activities		
		Business Objectives	Performance Measures	
			Targets	
		Organisation Structure	Organisational Unit	
Centralised enterprise documentation	Strategic Plan	Business Objectives	Performance Measures	
			Targets	
		Strategic Initiatives		
	Business Plan	Activities		
		Business Objectives	Performance Measures	
			Targets	

Information Flow	Data and/or Documentation	Data and/or Documentation	Data and/or Documentation	Data and/or Documentation
		Organisation Structure	Organisational Unit	
	Workforce Plan			
	Security Plan			
	Knowledge Management Plan			
Current SBT architecture and assessment	Current Architecture Assessment	Current Architecture	Business Architecture	Transition Plan
				Activity Model
				Process Model
				Business Reference Model
				Value Chain
				Business Services Model
			IT Systems Architecture	Systems Model
				System Function Model
				Service Reference Model
			Network Architecture	Networks Model
			Strategy Architecture	Strategic Plan
				Integrated Balance Scorecard
				SWOT Analysis
			Data Architecture	Data Model
				Information Exchange
			Security Architecture	Security Plan

Information Flow	Data and/or Documentation	Data and/or Documentation	Data and/or Documentation	Data and/or Documentation
			Workforce Architecture	Organisation Structure
				Workforce Plan
				Knowledge and Skills
			Standards Architecture	Technical Service Standards Profile
				Technical Service Standards Forecast
		SWOT Analysis	Influence	
		Performance Gap Analysis	Performance Measures	
	Performance Gap Analysis	Performance Measures		
Current activities and information flows	Activity Model	Activities		
		Information Exchange		
		Business Services		
		Needline		
	Information Exchange			
EA management plan	EA Management Plan	Transition Plan	Investment	Timing
				Dependencies
				Issues
				Activities
EA maturity assessment	EA Audit Report	EA Audit Dimension		
		EA Audit Dimension Score		

Information Flow	Data and/or Documentation	Data and/or Documentation	Data and/or Documentation	Data and/or Documentation
EA reference models	Reference Model	Business Reference Model		
		Data Reference Model		
		Service Reference Model		
		Technical Reference Model		
EA standards forecast	Technical Service Standards Forecast	Technical Reference Model		
EA standards profile	Technical Service Standards Profile	Technology		
		Technical Reference Model		
Existing investment portfolio	Project Portfolio	Investment	Timing	
			Dependencies	
			Issues	
			Activities	
		Project Overview	Technology Solution Design	Technology
				Systems Functions
				System Data Exchange
				Application
				Computer
				Network Components
			Investment Business Case	Technology Solution Design
				Investment
				Business Objectives

Information Flow	Data and/or Documentation	Data and/or Documentation	Data and/or Documentation	Data and/or Documentation
			Business Objectives	Performance Measures
				Targets
Future SB&T architecture documentation	Future Architecture	Business Architecture	Transition Plan	Investment
			Activity Model	Activities
				Information Exchange
				Business Services
				Needline
			Process Model	Activities
			Business Reference Model	
			Value Chain	Activities
			Business Services Model	Business Services
				Needline
				Customer
				Partner
		IT Systems Architecture	Systems Model	Application
			System Function Model	Systems Functions
			Service Reference Model	
		Network Architecture	Networks Model	Computer
				Network Components
		Strategy Architecture	Strategic Plan	Business Objectives
				Strategic Initiatives
				Business Objectives

Information Flow	Data and/or Documentation	Data and/or Documentation	Data and/or Documentation	Data and/or Documentation
			Integrated Balanced Scorecard	Perspective
				Strategic Initiatives
			SWOT Analysis	Influence
		Data Architecture	Data Model	Entity
			Information Exchange	
		Security Architecture	Security Plan	
		Workforce Architecture	Organisation Structure	Organisational Unit
			Workforce Plan	
			Knowledge and Skills	
		Standards Architecture	Technical Service Standards Profile	Technology
				Technical Reference Model
			Technical Service Standards Forecast	Technical Reference Model
Investment business case	Investment Business Case	Technology Solution Design	Technology	
			Systems Functions	
			System Data Exchange	
			Application	
			Computer	
			Network Components	
		Investment	Timing	
			Dependencies	
			Issues	
			Activities	

Information Flow	Data and/or Documentation	Data and/or Documentation	Data and/or Documentation	Data and/or Documentation
		Business Objectives	Performance Measures	
			Targets	
Knowledge management plan	Knowledge Management Plan			
Public modelling standards	EA Modelling Guidelines			
Security plans, standards and procedures	Security Plan			
Strategic drivers and directions	Strategic Plan	Business Objectives	Performance Measures	
			Targets	
		Strategic Initiatives		
	Integrated Balanced Scorecard	Business Objectives	Performance Measures	
			Targets	
		Perspective		
		Strategic Initiatives		
	SWOT Analysis	Influence		
Technology solution assessment	Technology Solution Alignment Assessment	Investment		
		EA Component		
Technology solution design	Technology Solution Design	Technology		
		Systems Functions		
		System Data Exchange		
		Application		
		Computer		
		Network Components		

Information Flow	Data and/or Documentation	Data and/or Documentation	Data and/or Documentation	Data and/or Documentation
Technology trends				

What rules are associated with the data in the core mission activity information flows?

To fully support the EA customers' corporate and IT governance questions, relationships between the various enterprise components need to be understood so that they can be gathered, managed, analysed and reported upon. The relationships in the EA data model are based on the linkages that are required to be understood if they are to highlight how the components at each layer of the framework impact or use, address or fulfil, support or implement components in the same or higher layer of the framework.

Described in terms of a Unified Modelling Language (UML) Class diagram, Figure 15 illustrates the core data concepts of EA and their relationships. The concepts are overlaid on the framework layers to help define the purpose, intent and order of derivation and requirement. For descriptions of the core concepts illustrated, refer to the Appendix – The EA Data Dictionary and Glossary.

As these core data and relationship concepts represent both the key enterprise components to be documented when doing EA for an enterprise, and the reference architecture documents an EA function based on the concepts described by the reference architecture, then the components documented in the reference architecture are examples of these data and relationships.

Figure 15: Enterprise Component Conceptual Data Model (Artefact D-5)

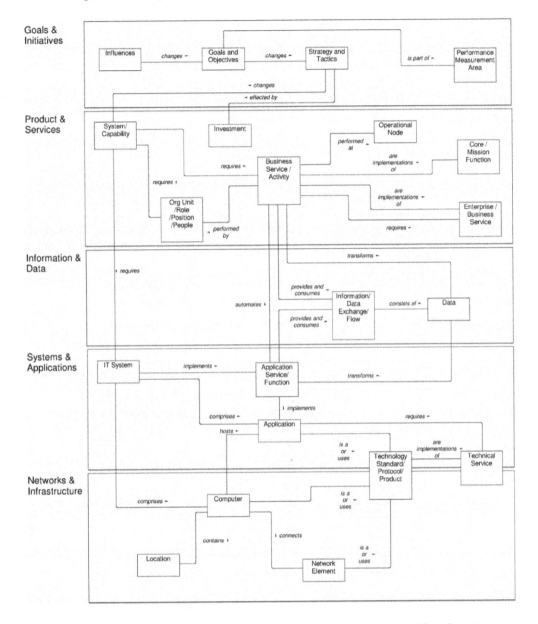

How is the documentation and data consumed and produced by the EA function best categorised?

Information is generally divided into different categories reflecting such things as content, format, granularity, use, lifecycle, etc. Identifying the different types or categories of information an enterprise uses helps to identify the data and information management activities likely to be performed, the types of information technologies required to support these, and to prioritise which activities and technologies are of greatest relevance or importance.

In Table 13 the documentation and data consumed and provided by the core mission EA activities have been categorised into 4 types. These categories have been selected based on the granularity, level of integration and the level of assessment that is captured or represented by the documentation and data. All of which are key and common attributes of EA documentation and data.

Table 13: Data and Documentation Categories

Category	Description
Enterprise Component	Documentation describing in detail an instance of a particular type of enterprise component. Including its definition, classifications and inter-relationships.
Primitive Artefact	Graphical or textual documentation representing one or more instances of a particular type of enterprise component that is used to aid understanding and communication.
Composite Artefact	Documentation containing the results of a process of analysis, design, deployment or operations, for example, a strategic plan, knowledge management plan, business case, etc. Generally they contain a combination of unstructured or textual information, models and component data and views that collectively outline some direction or process.
Management View	A graphical or textual representation of one or more instances of one or more types of enterprise components that is derived from the data in the models and component documentation, and aimed at addressing a particular EA customer's question about the enterprise to support their corporate and/or IT governance functions/management processes.

What types of information flows require automation to maximise the performance of the EA function?

The key EA documentation and data supporting the core mission activities of the EA function are those about the enterprise's strategy, business and technology components. This information is sourced from across the enterprise, from many and varied sources, and needs to be integrated and massaged to support analysis and ease of access and use in support of planning and oversight decision-making.

Automation of information flows comes in many forms:

- Data capture and synchronisation of inputs
- Information management techniques for publishing, charting and reporting of outputs
- Simulations, calculations and modelling for transforming data.

Lack of accurate and complete data about the enterprise across the framework layers can narrow the planning and oversight decision-making, resulting in missed opportunities or priorities and negatively impacting communications between various parts of the enterprise. Also, complete and accurate information that takes too much time to capture or refresh can negatively impact a business's ability to respond to its changing environment. Information flows containing data about strategy, business and technology components are therefore prime candidates for input automation.

Documentation of implicit and explicit links between modelled components is key to meeting line of sight, traceability and impact view and analysis requirements. They support the identification, agreement and communication of changes through the layers of the enterprise. Like data about the components themselves, limits to the completeness, accuracy and timeliness of the capture and refresh of linkage information will limit an organisation's alignment, agility and assurance. Automation support for the linking of component documentation and data is therefore also important to maximising EA performance.

Provision of useful information to EA customers to help improve their performance and decision-making is key to meeting many of the customer objectives. Automation that presents and publishes the EA current and future state architecture views and the EA management plan in a useful and accessible way to communicate, direct and control changes to the enterprise, is therefore important for automation.

In summary, the key automation requirements are those that will:

- Allow timely, complete, and accurate capture and linking of the incoming documentation and data
- Provide ease of access and usability of outgoing information flows used in decision-making.

What types of knowledge management solutions are applicable to the automation of the EA information flows?

Knowledge Management (KM)[3] is a concept wherein an enterprise consciously and comprehensively gathers, organises, shares, and analyses its knowledge in terms of data and information, as well as resources, capabilities, and activities. KM involves both 'pulling' (data mining) and 'pushing' (data marts) data and information to internal and external customers in ways that seamlessly provide and present data and information from multiple sources (FUN, EATP).

Critical success factors for KM include:

- *A KM strategy and plan that is aligned with the strategic plan and business plans and is supported by executive and LOB managers*
- *Data standards for entities and objects that enable seamless exchanges between different databases, applications, and websites*
- *EA artefacts that provide a clear understanding of strategic goals and business requirements for information flows within/between LOBs*
- *KM applications, best practices and trained personnel to enable the implementation and ongoing maintenance of the KM strategy/plan.*

Maximising access to and use of EA documentation and data is a key tenet of many of the EA objectives. A repository of EA data that is a single place for the storage, retrieval, analysis and reporting of EA artefacts is a critical component of any communications improvement solution.

Furthermore, on the topic of an EA repository, Dr Scott Bernard states: 'A repository works best if it is easy to access and use. For this reason, an online, web-based EA repository is recommended. This type of web 'portal' for EA should be located on the enterprise's internal Local Area Network to promote security of the information while still supporting access by executives, managers and staff. Sensitive EA information should be stored in a separate repository or available from the general repository through access control.' (FUN, EATP)

Represented as a 'concept of operations' diagram (FUN, EATP), the key components of the automation solutions for the EA function is provided in Figure 16.

---

[3] Also commonly referred to as Information Management.

Figure 16: EA Repository and Tools Concept of Operations (Artefact D-1)

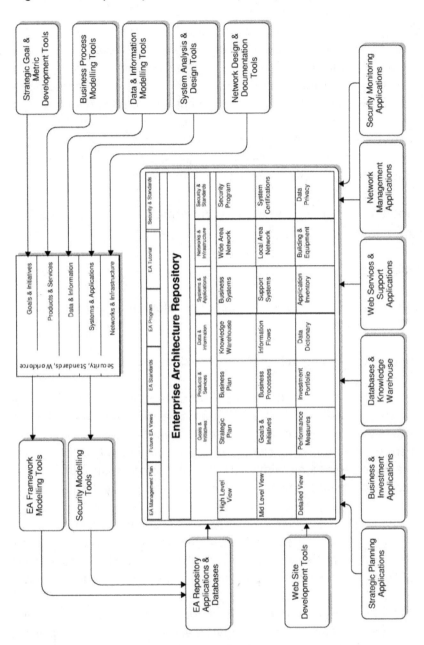

In brief, the concept of operations is as follows:

- Modelling tools are required to capture the various enterprise component data and documentation and to populate the EA repository.
- An EA framework modelling tool is required to help massage, integrate and analyse the data and documentation.

- Security Modelling tools are required to expand on the security aspects of the component data and documentation.
- Various website development tools are required to help present the component data and documentation, and the results of the massaging, integration and analysis, in a useable and accessible way through an EA portal.
- Documentation and data resident in other applications that make up parts of the enterprise's architecture and are not populated in the EA repository are made accessible via the EA portal. This ensures a complete picture of the enterprise at the various required levels of detail.
- The EA portal is promoted as the primary source of information for data and documentation about the enterprise's architecture.

What should be considered when documenting and analysing the Data and Information layer?

For an Enterprise

When documenting and assessing the Data and Information layer of the enterprise, consider the following:

1. **Data and Information is part of the Business domain**

   It may be a cliché, but data and information is an integral part of doing business today. And it is the business people who know what data and information is needed, and how and when it is needed to allow them to perform their duties efficiently. They are also normally more than aware of the issues associated with their data and information that are hampering their performance, having to live with them on a daily basis.

   In many cases, however, they either don't have the background, knowledge or time to keep up with the data and information practices and technologies that implement the governance activities and provide the functionality that will optimise the usefulness and accessibility of data and information.

   This layer provides an opportunity to focus on gaining a better understanding of the needs of an enterprise's services and activities by focusing on their data and information requirements. These requirements include the performance implications of the current data and information used and available by data consumer activities, and the content, timeliness, accuracy, completeness of the data and information needed to achieve business objectives

2. Data and information requirements are relatively stable

Advances in information technology provide increasing numbers of opportunities to improve business performance and competiveness. Greater numbers of channels to service customers or citizens, improved business insights and analytics, and improved collaboration and sharing, being cases in point. However, in the most part, the data and information being shared or analysed in all these cases remains essentially the same.

In this layer, try to draw out the data and information requirements and characteristics independent of implementation or technology. This will help to focus solutions on meeting the needs of the business and their partners and building data and documentation of an enterprise's data and information requirements that aids communicating, describing and documenting solutions in terms of business needs and requirements rather than their solutions. That is, decoupling need from solution and allowing the gap between current solution and need to be more clearly defined and addressed.

3. Information exchanges drive data requirements

Making data and information available to the right people, at the right time and at the right place is key to understanding data and information services, transfers and transforms, and supporting application and technology requirements.

As such, while structure helps us to understand the real world entities for which data and information is being managed and shared and the rules that are to be associated with and to be imposed on these entities, it is the inter and intra data and information flows that determine what data and information is needed and how and where the data and information is to be held, transformed and presented to support these exchanges.

4. Risks to the business and its customers and citizens are key drivers of data and information requirements

Providing access to data and information to consumers is becoming easier and cheaper. For example, getting data and information up on the Internet or to consumers via mobile devices is possible for nearly all organisations, large and small, for relatively low cost.

Ease of access and provision of data and information, however, is only one aspect of data and information management that enterprises need to consider. Access alone won't win and retain customers, and without the right safeguards in place can expose organisations and their customers or citizens to an increasing level of security and fraud risk.

Many technology solutions are therefore driven by the problems associated with the management of data and information with a view to addressing one or more of the following, and to a level appropriate to its importance:

o	Usability	The ease in which to navigate and consume data and information
o	Accessibility	Access to the right data by the right people
o	Completeness	Enough data and information on which to base decisions and do business
o	Accuracy	Reliable and consistent data and information on which to base decisions and do business
o	Frequency	Availability of the right data at the right time

Documentation of an enterprise's data and information requirements should be considered incomplete unless consideration is given to the gaps between the current and required states of information flows against one or all of the above.

5. **Data and information requirements help to balance and develop the objectives of the previous two layers**

Quantified improvements in the frequency, accuracy, completeness, accessibility and usability of data and information are typical internal process objectives as part of the Balanced Scorecard and Strategy Map approach.

Like the objectives derived during the documentation and analysis of the Products and Services layer, measurable information improvements further help to balance and develop the strategy of the enterprise.

As with the approach adopted in the Products and Services layer, information improvement objectives should be fed back up to the Goal and Initiatives layer, and either aggregated into a single enterprise Balanced Scorecard or separated into line of business-specific Balanced Scorecards, with common or shared objectives and initiatives present on all.

6. The Corporate Data Model and EA

Many potential benefits are attributed to Corporate Data Models. Unfortunately, many organisations have expended too much effort attempting to document a single data model of critical business data rules and classifications without any perceivable benefit to the organisation.

One of the main reasons for this failure has been the stand-alone nature of corporate data modelling exercises. Without context, for example, understanding of usage, implementations, performance issues, and if unable to consistently and easily use and refer to the corporate data model, various potential consumers of the model will quickly resort to describing data and information relevant to their undertaking in terms expedient or related to their task.

One of the objectives of EA is to improve coherency across an organisation by helping the business and IT governance functions and management process to discuss the components of the enterprise using a single taxonomy and glossary of terms. The corporate data model provides this for the data and information components in the Data and Information layer.

EA is also responsible for documenting and analysing changeable components across business and IT in support of its improved planning and oversight objectives, in particular, capturing the implicit and explicit links between changeable components that allows for improved analysis. Providing the means for the corporate data model to be integrated with other changeable components, for example, the processes that use the data it describes, the applications that transform the data it describes, and the information flows that move the data it describes, providing the context previously missing.

As such, EA addresses many of the factors that have previously prevented realisation of the benefits associated with a corporate data model.

For the EA Function

When using the reference architecture to document and assess the EA function's data and information layer:

1. **Good and proper EA define the full set of data requirements; EA Services prioritise EA data requirement capture and usage**

    A core concept of EA is the integration of data and documentation about the changeable components within the enterprise in support of various governance activities. Good and proper EA requires data and documentation about changeable components from strategic, business and technology perspectives.

    While some EA services can be delivered and governance activities supported with data and documentation about some but not all of the changeable components, the long-term goal should be to gather, manage and use data and documentation for all changeable components.

    Early EA function activities should endeavour to contribute to building the full set of data and documentation in such a way that it is reusable and sharable with and between the various integration governance activities.

2. **Key EA data and information drivers**

    Use the agreed list of EA services to help scope and prioritise the data and documentation required to be delivered or assessed by the EA function.

    Use the information flows to help identify the required input documentation and data in the enterprise and the likely sources or providers of this type of information.

    Determine the gap between the resultant list of required input and output data and documentation items and that currently available in the EA function and the broader enterprise. Scoring each information flow and data and documentation item in terms of the characteristics discussed above for an enterprise in the 'Risk to the business and its customers/citizens are key drivers of data' section.

    This will provide the documentation for and assessment of the current state of the EA function from a data and information perspective and will help define the plans and targets for the EA function in terms of information flow management effort.

3. **The EA Corporate Data Model**

The EA data and information layer's data model is the corporate data model of the EA function. Given the nature of EA, this means that it should also be promoted as the terms of reference to be used to describe architectural components for which data and documentation is collected and shared with all other functions within the broader enterprise. Therefore, while it must reflect the data requirements to support the EA objectives, it equally should be accessible and non-confrontational by the providers and consumers of EA data and documentation.

Use the documented EA data model as the starting point for the EA functions data model or, alternatively, as a reference model to ensure completeness and coverage of the data and relationships to be maintained by your EA function.

Publish the EA data model along with aliases, meaningful and illustrative descriptions and enterprise segment-specific views, as required, and set it up to be the terms of reference for the enterprise.

4. **Treat EA Documentation and Data As An Asset**

Allowing EA data and information to continue to build and grow and to extend its ability to meet EA management process requirements and EA customer needs, as promoted by the reference architecture, requires that it is treated as more than just temporary, project-based work products that can be archived, destroyed or ignored once their immediate use is over.

This requires applying typical knowledge/information management planning and techniques to EA documentation, no different to that used for documentation and data within the broader enterprise.

Develop a Knowledge Management Plan for EA documentation and data that takes into account:

- o The recommended practices, tooling, and standards for knowledge and information management for other activities within the enterprise
- o The EA service, information flow and documentation and data management-specific and unique requirements.

Section 4 – The Systems and Applications of the EA function

Based on the EA[3] approach, in the Systems and Applications layer of the framework it is important to ask:

- Which IT systems and services will be needed to generate, share, and store the data, information, and knowledge that the business processes need?
- How can multiple types of IT systems, services, applications, databases, and websites be made to work together where needed?
- How can configuration management help to create a cost-effective and operationally efficient 'Common Operating Environment' for IT services?
- What are the workforce, standards, and security issues at these levels?

From an EA function perspective, this section aims to identify and describe the types of systems, system functionality and system services that are required to automate and support the effective management of EA documentation and data in support of the delivery of EA services and activities. For example, the EA data and information capture, review and analysis functions or the data and information sharing and reporting automations and services.

What are the core mission system functions necessary to support the management of the EA documentation and data as well as the EA program-specific data?

The complexity and amount of documentation and data that the EA function needs to gather, interpret, link, analyse, assess, summarise, socialise and publish is not insignificant. Described as a functional decomposition, Figure 17 illustrates the key types of system functions required to provide the automation necessary for the effective capture, transformation and exchange of this data and documentation. Each leaf level system function is described in Table 14.

The EA system functions were derived from an assessment of:

- The classes of documentation and data consumed and provided by the EA function
- The type of operations performed on the documentation and data by the EA function and its customers and/or partners
- The knowledge management concept of operations for EA documentation and data management, sharing and presentation.

To reduce the complexity and number of system functions, the EA system functions are described in terms of the categories of documentation and data, e.g., component or composite, as opposed to the specific types of documentation and data, e.g., objective, activity, application, computer, etc., being captured, transformed and exchanged.

Figure 17: EA System Functions (Artefact SA-4)

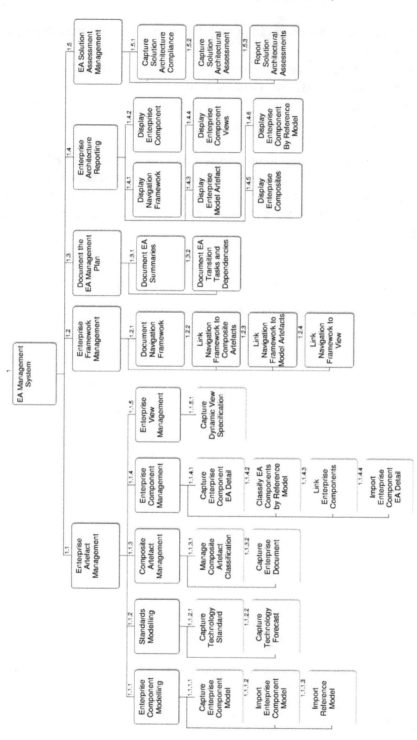

Table 14: Leaf System Function Purpose (Artefact SA-4)

#	EA System Function	Purpose
1.1.1.1	Capture Enterprise Component Model	Capture of the graphical representations of enterprise components necessary to support the communications and understanding of the enterprise's architecture.
1.1.1.2	Import Enterprise Component Model	Automation of the collection of component models from alternative modelling systems.
1.1.1.3	Import Reference Model	Automation of the collection of an enterprise reference model.
1.1.2.1	Capture Technology Standard	Allows for the current standards of technology services to be captured to support decision-making during planning and change activities.
1.1.2.2	Capture Technology Forecast	Allows results of an assessment of a technical service to be captured for future reference.
1.1.3.1	Manage Composite Artefact Classification	Allows the set-up and maintenance of a classification scheme that will allow the differentiation and ease of identification of composite artefact content and relevance.
1.1.3.2	Capture Enterprise Document	Allows an electronic document to be input into an application so it can be easily found and retrieved via a service or programmatic interface.
1.1.4.1	Capture Enterprise Component EA Detail	To capture a representation of an EA component and the detail important to the mission and vision of the EA.
1.1.4.2	Classify EA Components by Reference Model	Allows the enterprise components captured to be classified against the reference models for duplicate process and resource identification.
1.1.4.3	Link Enterprise Components	Allows the integration of the strategy, business and technology enterprise components.
1.1.4.4	Import Enterprise Component EA Detail	Automation of the collection of EA significant details from system sources.
1.1.5.1	Capture Dynamic View Specification	Supports the construction of queries and the specification of the output requirements to support the production of views to answer EA customer questions.
1.2.1	Document Navigation Framework	Allows the set-up and maintenance of the portal that will facilitate end user navigation and location of the

#	EA System Function	Purpose
		enterprise views, composites, models, etc. they require.
1.2.2	Link Navigation Framework to Composite Artefacts	Allows the establishment of the rules for retrieving composite artefacts via the enterprise navigation framework.
1.2.3	Link Navigation Framework to Model Artefacts	Allows the establishment of the rules for retrieving model artefacts via the enterprise navigation framework.
1.2.4	Link Navigation Framework to View	Allows views to be accessed via the navigation framework.
1.3.1	Document EA Summaries	Allows the results of analysis of the architecture to be captured in a simpler format than the composites, models and detail.
1.3.2	Document EA Transition Tasks and Dependencies	Allows the scheduling of investments into a form suitable for communicating the timeframes and dependencies of the transition investments.
1.4.1	Display Navigation Framework	Allows an end user to view and locate the EA content of import to the duties.
1.4.2	Display Enterprise Component	Allows the data describing an enterprise component to be presented.
1.4.3	Display Enterprise Model Artefact	Allows a model artefact to be retrieved and presented to an end user.
1.4.4	Display Enterprise Component Views	Allows the generation of a graphical or textual presentation of enterprise architecture components based on their classifications, linkages and descriptive detail.
1.4.5	Display Enterprise Composites	Allows a composite artefact to be retrieved and presented to an end user.
1.4.6	Display Enterprise Component By Reference Model	Displays the enterprise components that have been associated to each of the items with the selected reference models and/or reference item.
1.5.1	Capture Solution Architecture Compliance	Capture of scope, objectives, compliance and divergence of a solution to the planned and target architecture.
1.5.2	Capture Solution Architectural Assessment	Allows the results of the assessment of a solution architecture against the standards, models and plans to be input and managed.
1.5.3	Report Solution Architectural Assessments	Lists the results of the assessment of a solution architecture for sharing and discussion.

How are the system functions to be used by the core mission and support EA activities?

Across all organisations access to a range of different automations and system functions is required to support the optimal delivery of its services and the performance of its activities. Some of these system functions may be required or used by more than one activity, while others will be specific to individual activities. To get a view of specific usage patterns for system functionality, the opportunities for reuse and/or rationalisation of system function implementations and the under supported priority activities, a system function to activity matrix is commonly used.

Described in terms of such a matrix, in Table 15 the EA Management System's system functions that are of prime importance to each of the EA function's activities are mapped.

Table 15: System Function to Internal Activities Matrix (Artefact SA-5)

#	System Function	EA Reference Model Review and Update	Standards Identification and Consolidation	Standards Forecasting	Identify and Review Existing Documentation	Document and Assess Current Architecture	Document and Review Future Scenarios	Document Future Architecture	Document the EA Summaries and Sequence Plan	Provide Planning Support	Provide Resource Management Support	Assess Business Case Solutions	Oversee Technology Solution	Provide Change Support	EA Tool and Repository Planning	EA Tool and Repository Configuration	EA Tool and Repository Upgrade	EA Program Reporting	EA Team Management	EA Maturity Assessment	EA Communications Plan Creation and Update
1.1.1.1	Capture Enterprise Component Model					X	X	X													
1.1.1.2	Import Enterprise Component Model					X															
1.1.1.3	Import Reference Model	X																			

#	EA Activity (Internal) / System Function	EA Reference Model Review and Update	Standards Identification and Consolidation	Standards Forecasting	Identify and Review Existing Documentation	Document and Assess Current Architecture	Document and Review Future Scenarios	Document Future Architecture	Document the EA Summaries and Sequence Plan	Provide Planning Support	Provide Resource Management Support	Assess Business Case Solutions	Oversee Technology Solution	Provide Change Support	EA Tool and Repository Planning	EA Tool and Repository Configuration	EA Tool and Repository Upgrade	EA Program Reporting	EA Team Management	EA Maturity Assessment	EA Communications Plan Creation and Update
1.1.2.1	Capture Technology Standard		X																		
1.1.2.2	Capture Technology Forecast			X																	
1.1.3.1	Manage Composite Artefact Classification															X					
1.1.3.2	Capture Enterprise Document	X	X	X	X	X			X		X										X
1.1.4.1	Capture Enterprise Component EA Detail					X		X	X												
1.1.4.2	Classify EA Components by Reference Model										X										
1.1.4.3	Link Enterprise Components					X		X	X												
1.1.4.4	Import Enterprise Component EA Detail					X															

#	System Function	EA Reference Model Review and Update	Standards Identification and Consolidation	Standards Forecasting	Identify and Review Existing Documentation	Document and Assess Current Architecture	Document and Review Future Scenarios	Document Future Architecture	Document the EA Summaries and Sequence Plan	Provide Planning Support	Provide Resource Management Support	Assess Business Case Solutions	Oversee Technology Solution	Provide Change Support	EA Tool and Repository Planning	EA Tool and Repository Configuration	EA Tool and Repository Upgrade	EA Program Reporting	EA Team Management	EA Maturity Assessment	EA Communications Plan Creation and Update
1.1.5.1	Capture Dynamic View Specification															X					
1.2.1	Document Navigation Framework															X					
1.2.2	Link Navigation Framework to Composite Artefacts															X					
1.2.3	Link Navigation Framework to Model Artefacts															X					
1.2.4	Link Navigation Framework to View															X					
1.3.1	Document EA Summaries								X												
1.3.2	Document EA Transition Tasks and Dependencies								X												
1.4.1	Display Navigation Framework		X			X		X	X												
1.4.2	Display Enterprise Component		X			X		X	X			X	X								

#	EA Activity (Internal) / System Function	EA Reference Model Review and Update	Standards Identification and Consolidation	Standards Forecasting	Identify and Review Existing Documentation	Document and Assess Current Architecture	Document and Review Future Scenarios	Document Future Architecture	Document the EA Summaries and Sequence Plan	Provide Planning Support	Provide Resource Management Support	Assess Business Case Solutions	Oversee Technology Solution	Provide Change Support	EA Tool and Repository Planning	EA Tool and Repository Configuration	EA Tool and Repository Upgrade	EA Program Reporting	EA Team Management	EA Maturity Assessment	EA Communications Plan Creation and Update
1.4.3	Display Enterprise Model Artefact		X			X			X	X		X	X								
1.4.4	Display Enterprise Component Views		X			X			X	X		X	X								
1.4.5	Display Enterprise Composites					X			X			X	X								
1.4.6	Display Enterprise Component By Reference Model										X										
1.5.1	Capture Solution Architecture Compliance																				
1.5.2	Capture Solution Architectural Assessment											X	X								
1.5.3	Report Solution Architectural Assessments												X								

From the matrix, it is possible to see the system functions responsible for displaying data and capturing enterprise documentation are the most widely used internally by the EA function. From the matrix it is also easy to see the grouping of system functions specific to the core mission activities of the EA function and those specific to its support activities.

How will the system functions support the EA function's customers and partner activities?

To best support the performance of EA customers and partners the provision of EA documentation, assessments and plans are critical success factors. System functionality or automations that make these as easy to access and as usable as possible in support of their activities are the focus here.

Described in terms of a matrix, Table 16 illustrates the EA Management System's system functions of primary importance to the governance functions and management processes that the EA function integrates with and considered its customers and partners. The matrix thus highlights key EA function's system functions and automations required to optimise the information flows to its customers and partners.

Table 16: System Function to External Activities Matrix (Artefact SA-5)

#	System Function	Strategic Planning	Business Planning	System Development	Information Management	Capital Planning	Business Operations	IT Lifecycle/Change Management	Program Monitoring	Planning and Oversight	Industry Standards Determination	Practice Engineering	Technology Analysis	Security Planning
1.1.2.1	Capture Technology Standard										X			
1.1.2.2	Capture Technology Forecast												X	
1.4.1	Display Navigation Framework	X	X	X	X	X	X			X	X		X	
1.4.2	Display Enterprise Component	X	X	X	X	X	X			X			X	

#	System Function	Strategic Planning	Business Planning	System Development	Information Management	Capital Planning	Business Operations	IT Lifecycle/Change Management	Program Monitoring	Planning and Oversight	Industry Standards Determination	Practice Engineering	Technology Analysis	Security Planning
1.4.3	Display Enterprise Model Artefact	X	X	X	X	X	X			X			X	
1.4.4	Display Enterprise Component Views	X	X	X	X	X	X			X	X		X	
1.4.5	Display Enterprise Composites	X	X	X	X	X	X			X			X	
1.4.6	Display Enterprise Component By Reference Model									X	X		X	
1.5.1	Capture Solution Architectural Assessment			X										
1.5.2	Report Solution Architectural Assessments			X		X		X		X				X
1.5.3	Report Performance Measures Status								X					

From the matrix, it is possible to again see the importance of the 'Display' system functions to the delivery of EA value. Another highlight is the inclusion of system functionality for the capture and reporting of solution architecture and standards compliance assessments. By providing automation support in this area the method by which solution architecture and standards compliance assessment are performed and evaluated can be optimised, which should in turn improve the alignment and fit-for purpose of solutions through greater transparency into, and better informed, decision-making within project or solution teams.

What application and technology component alternatives are available to implement the core mission system functions?

In keeping with the EA Knowledge Management Plan proposed earlier, to maximise EA function and EA customer performance a sophisticated tooling and repository solution is considered a core element and critical success factor of the EA function defined by the reference architecture.

The systems or applications procured or developed within an organisation to implement the various types of system functions that it requires, however, often depend on many factors. For the EA function these factors are principally, the:

- Core focus and governance support services planned for the EA function. Refer to Section 9 – The EA Program and Transition Plan section for a discussion on this and
- Maturity of the EA function, i.e., artefacts under management, core elements in place, ability to repeat documentation and assessments activities, etc.
- Availability and depth of skills within the team
- Available of funds and resources to undertake EA activities.

In order to reflect this variation in practice, in Table 17, tooling approaches often encountered in organisations to meet the EA system functional requirements have been provided for three levels of EA maturity and/or technology sophistication.

The mistake that is often made and to be avoided is prolonging the use of early maturity and/or low technology sophistication tooling or methods or not treating the EA tool and repository as a core element during EA function establishment because, as has been discussed throughout the book, optimised access and use of EA documentation and analysis is critical to the meeting the service delivery objectives of the EA function and the performance objectives of the EAs customers and partners.

Table 17: Core Mission System Function Alternatives (Artefact SA-7)

System Function	Early Maturity and/or Low Technology Sophistication	Mid Maturity and/or Medium Technology Sophistication	Mature and/or High Technology Sophistication
Enterprise Component Modelling	Office tools	Standalone/Point, or Enterprise, Modelling Tools	Enterprise Modelling Tools and/or EA Management Suites
Enterprise Component Management		Database	
Enterprise Architecture Reporting	Static and handcrafted reports	Reporting tools	Dynamic access to reports
Importing Functions	Manual	Partially Automated	Fully Automated

System Function	Early Maturity and/or Low Technology Sophistication	Mid Maturity and/or Medium Technology Sophistication	Mature and/or High Technology Sophistication
Composite Artefacts Management	File server		Document Management
Solution Architecture Assessment	Office tools		Single Point of Entry to EA System

What are the system function deployment requirements to be supported?

Across any enterprise different roles require access to different system functions at different points within a process. These systems functions provide automations and facilitate flows of data and information specific to the activity that the role is performing. The geographical or organisational location of roles may impose particular technical and communications requirements on the delivery or implementation of the system function. It is therefore important to not only consider what automations and/or data and/or information is required by an activity but also where they are required.

To facilitate the effective management and use of EA documentation and data discussed in earlier sections, different EA system functionality, depending on EA documentation and data responsibilities and requirements, will need to be deployed or made accessible to EA stakeholders internal and external to the EA function that will be located in different areas of the enterprise.

In keeping with the artefact notation standards defined as part of the reference architecture, the physical or figurative locations where system functions are likely to be required, i.e., to be deployed or accessed, are referred to as system nodes.

Described in matrix form, in Table 18 the EA Management System's system functions have been mapped against several types of system node to help plan and understand the physical distribution requirements of each EA system function. Each system node representing a type of EA stakeholder and described as a desktop to highlight the physical nature of the distribution and/or accessibility requirement.

Table 18: EA System Function to System Node)

#	System Function	Domain Architect Desktop	EA Customer Desktop	EA Program Managers Desktop	Enterprise Architect Desktop	Solution Architecture Desktop	Technology Architect Desktop	Tool Administrator Desktop
1.1.1.1	Capture Enterprise Component Model	X					X	
1.1.1.2	Import Enterprise Component Model				X			
1.1.1.3	Import Reference Model				X			
1.1.2.1	Capture Technology Standard	X			X		X	
1.1.2.2	Capture Technology Forecast						X	
1.1.3.1	Manage Composite Artefact Classification							
1.1.3.2	Capture Enterprise Document	X					X	
1.1.4.1	Capture Enterprise Component EA Detail	X					X	
1.1.4.2	Classify EA Components by Reference Model	X					X	
1.1.4.3	Link Enterprise Components	X			X			
1.1.4.4	Import Enterprise Component EA Detail				X			
1.1.5.1	Capture Dynamic View Specification							
1.2.1	Document Navigation Framework				X			
1.2.2	Link Navigation Framework to Composite Artefacts				X			
1.2.3	Link Navigation Framework to Model Artefacts				X			
1.2.4	Link Navigation Framework to View				X			
1.3.1	Document EA Summaries				X			
1.3.2	Document EA Transition Tasks and Dependencies				X			
1.4.1	Display Navigation Framework	X	X					
1.4.2	Display Enterprise Component	X	X					
1.4.3	Display Enterprise Model Artefact	X						
1.4.4	Display Enterprise Component Views	X	X					
1.4.5	Display Enterprise Composites	X						

#	System Function	Domain Architect Desktop	EA Customer Desktop	EA Program Managers Desktop	Enterprise Architect Desktop	Solution Architecture Desktop	Technology Architect Desktop	Tool Administrator Desktop
1.4.6	Display Enterprise Component By Reference Model	X					X	
1.5.1	Capture Solution Architecture Compliance					X		
1.5.2	Capture Solution Architectural Assessment				X			
1.5.3	Report Solution Architectural Assessments		X			X	X	

What should be considered when documenting and analysing the Systems and Applications layer?

For An Enterprise

When documenting and assessing the Systems and Applications layer of the enterprise, consider the following:

1. **Are we not simply doing IT Architecture?**

   EA, like most and many management processes, has evolved over time. IT Architecture, defined here as a disciplined approach to the planning and oversight of systems and applications within the enterprise, sounds like EA and is often confused as EA. IT Architecture, however, has never been a coherent approach and is loosely made up of the various individual 'sub-architectures' and practices undertaken by the various groups responsible for the planning, development and operations of the IT components under their responsibility.

   While the aim of the approach and style of EA outlined by the reference architecture is focused on improving IT planning and oversight, the point of difference is that EA endeavours to integrate IT and business governance functions and management processes around a single coherent data and documentation source. A source that covers both IT and business components against which they can all agree, confer and manage change. IT architecture on the other hand is largely exclusive and does not concern itself with providing such a data and documentation source.

That said, taking an EA approach to the IT architecture by focusing data and documentation capture and assessment efforts on the lower layers of the enterprise architecture is a relatively easy way to get started on EA. It will provide knowledge management benefits and improve coherency across the IT groups. It should not, however, be called EA until a strategic, business and technology perspective is being taken to the data and documentation efforts, which requires stepping out of IT and working with the business and delivering the types of EA products and services identified in earlier sections of the reference architecture.

2. **Are we not simply doing Application Portfolio Management?**

Application portfolio management (APM) has similar objectives to the planning and oversight responsibilities of EA. In fact, its planning focus is largely identical to the scope and intent of the Systems and Applications layer within an EA Management Plan.

APM differs from EA principally, however, in its approach to uncovering and explaining the architecturally significant strategic, business and technology drivers. APM relies more on the capture of the results of its subjective and/or objective analysis to support decision-making as opposed to managing and maintaining architectural data and documentation to back up 'line of sight' assessments, other dependency analysis and data and documentation coherency services.

APM also tends to vary from EA in that it is a tool for the sole purpose of assisting ICT groups in meeting their operational requirements as owners and managers of the portfolio of systems and applications on behalf of the 'business'. EA's planning responsibilities, on the other hand, attempt to balance the planning across all ICT components and all drivers that directly or indirectly impact IT decisions, that is, strategic, business and technology drivers.

Use APM where a well-developed discipline is required to focus solely on the assessment, planning and oversight of systems and applications on behalf of the organisation. Use APM supported by EA when the assessment and management of the systems and applications portfolio and results of the analysis need to be made transparent, visible and usable by other governance functions and management processes, and contribute to a single architecture repository.

3. **Why separate system and application requirements from Data and Information requirements?**

Application functionality is the most common expression and tangible representation of data and information requirements. Much planning of new IT functionality is described in terms of the functionality required for data to be managed and information to be created.

System and application functionality, however, is the description of the transformative requirement. That is, the functionality for facilitating complex and/or mundane integration, restructuring, calculating, deriving or presenting data in forms that support the performance of downstream and/or dependent business functions and activities.

Information and data flows, on the other hand, describe the format in which the downstream and/or dependent business functions expect their data and information to be in to maximise performance. For example, the content needed, the format it should be in, its minimum quality characteristics independent of their implementation.

For example, achieving an information flow today may involve multiple people, systems and/or applications but in the future may be able to be automated or improved through a) data and/or application integration, b) a single application or c) access through a mobile or consumer device. The information flow requirement may not have changed just its realisation. Information exchanges therefore tend to be more stable and span physical implementations.

This is not to say that both are not required. Understanding the current implementations of system functions, system functionality and service implementation alternatives available, and their proposed implementation against information flow requirements, provides the basis for the gap and options analysis necessary to decide on the level of automation support that is feasible and attainable given budget, time and resource constraints.

4. **The tactile nature of systems and applications can't be ignored**

Systems and applications are the principal contact point between users and technology; becoming an integral part of the day-to-day activities of staff across an enterprise. The impact of disruptions to availability, any degradation in performance or changes to appearance, form and/or function can, and are, acutely felt by individuals that use them.

Consequently, slight changes and improvements can make a remarkable difference to the performance of users in the delivery of their services, or performance of their activities. Behaviour of systems and applications, and the way that end users interact with their systems and applications are, therefore, of far more importance to them than how or what they are implemented in.

Enhancements that improve behaviour or the way one interacts with a system or application can therefore make a big difference. They can be 'low-hanging fruit', resulting in business performance improvements for relatively little cost and/or effort.

Focusing too much effort on enhancements at the expense of competing drivers can pull resources away from potentially greater opportunities, such as addressing business priorities, pursuing strategic directions, improving maintainability of systems, reducing complexity of systems, rationalising technologies or increasing component horizontalisation/reuse.

This is one of the critical areas, and benefits, that an EA approach to planning that Demand, Application and Portfolio management disciplines independently, or in isolation, struggle to address. That is, the visibility of competing drivers and their associated impacts and requirements across the enterprise, especially when there is a requirement to expend more effort on strategic initiatives.

As such, document and assess business performance issues associated with system and/or application functionality within the current state, identifying where possible any dependent or related components across all layers and threads that contribute to, or are the cause of, the performance issues. Determine whether an enhancement is warranted taking into account the status, plans, impacts and drivers on the component and its related components.

For the EA function

Using the reference architecture to document and assess the EA function's systems and applications layer:

1. **Do we really need a tool and repository for EA?**

   The amount of data and documentation to be managed, integrated, analysed, prepared and communicated can be significant. Several reference models of 10s or even 100s of definitions each, 100s and possibly 1000s of applications,

100s and possibly 1000s of types of technology, 100s and possible 1000s of business functions, etc. are not uncommon.

Good EAs and EA consultants, through a number of techniques such as those listed below can readily identify key or major changes with relatively ease. Allowing highly valuable EA Management Plans requiring little or no technology support, other than commonly-available office products, to be developed:

- Abstracting to tens of each of the core types of EA components,
- Use and application of planning and assessment frameworks
- Focusing on generalisations
- Highlighting 'low-hanging fruit', e.g. changes that are highly visible, easily understood, low cost and high value, and/or well supported or being pursued by management,

Also, good EAs through their in-depth knowledge, experience and understanding of the business and IT environments that they work in and their internal contacts and relationships can provide a high degree of consistency, direction and control during the planning and delivery of changes.

From an EA function development perspective, reliance on EAs and EA consultants alone should be considered a 'stop gap' measure or tactical solution and not a long term one. The lack of proper EA data and information supported by automation and the other core EA elements will ultimately lead to misinterpretation during implementation; greater rework and variance in planning and oversight; restricted and/or fewer integrated governance opportunities; and less data that can be classified as an asset. It also places the organisation at risk of sustaining a high degree of EA competence and EA service delivery, as the EAs and EA consultants have become 'single point of failure' and if they were too leave the EA function's capability to deliver will dramatically decrease, or at worse cease to exist.

As with any manual or office product-based process, tooling and automation involves an up-front cost and effort. The benefits of automating and tooling the EA function are however key to the delivery of the reference architecture's EA services. Automation and tooling therefore should be factored into the EA function if it is to meet the full spectrum of EA objectives and services, and to mitigate the risks associated with high dependency on EA human resources alone.

2. Assessing the implementations of current EA system functionality

Assessing the suitability of existing EA technology solutions comes down to measuring the performance of the EA function against its plans and objectives and determining how the existing solutions contribute are to their success. The results and targets from the assessment should feedback up as objectives and measures to the EA function's Goals and Initiatives layer, in particular the Learning and Growth perspective of the EA function's Balanced Scorecard.

The assessment of the technology solutions used or available to implement the EA system functions to support the EA function's performance and service delivery can and should be scored using the same international, national, or local – organisation-specific - standard or framework that is used for this purpose for the broader enterprise's systems and application.

In Table 19 the US Federal Segment Architecture Method (FSAM) system scorecard is provided as an example standard and framework for system assessment. It has been included due to its alignment with the EA[3] framework, in particular it support and reference to the same tiers, layers, threads and component names and definitions.

Table 19: US Federal Segment Architecture Method (FSAM) System Scorecard

Tier	Layer/Thread	Assessment
Strategy	Goals and Initiatives	System's capability for supporting associated Strategic goals and initiatives
		Extent of stakeholders' feedback for performance measurement and system refinement
		Demonstrate a projected return on investment that is clearly equal to or better than alternative uses of available resources (i.e. enterprise products or services)
Business	Products and Services	Lack of functional overlap with other systems
		System incorporates re-engineered/streamlined business processes (workflow) in an automated fashion
	Data and Information	Existence and documentation of data standards and quality control procedures
		Relative maturity of system's data storage and access methods
		Relative redundancy of system data

Tier	Layer/Thread	Assessment
		Existing Acquisition and Funding Strategy is appropriate to support mission needs as an enterprise service
		Existing Project/System(s) have been identified as candidate(s) for target Service needs
Technology	System and Application	Degree of enterprise architectural compliance
		Extent to which system design requirements are defined and documented
		Extent to which systems interfaces are defined and documented
		Extent to which high-level design or operational concepts are defined
		No alternative can efficiently support the function
	Networks and Infrastructure	Extent of compliance with Technology Reference Model standards, protocols and best practices
		Extent of maximum use of shared, existing infrastructure components and services
Thread	Security	Extent to which the system complies with current security requirements and extent of progress through the Certification and Accreditation (C&A) process
		System deployments are modular and are/have been performed in phases based on mission needs

3. Identifying target EA system functionality

The objectives in the EA function's Balanced Scorecard, Customer perspective and Internal Process perspective that were identified during the documentation and analysis of the Products and Services and Data and Information layers, and the results of the EA program planning covered in Section 9 - The EA Program and Transition Plan, will have identified and helped to prioritise particular EA services and activities for establishment and enablement.

Using the matrices in the Systems and Applications layer it will now be possible to identify the most important types of system functions required to support these.

However, due to the incremental and theme-based approach promoted or possible for EA Function establishment and enablement, and the method of documentation used to illustrate and define the EA system functions, many of the EA system functions will need to be repeatedly developed, or extended, to support and implement the full list of data and documentation, management and analysis requirements and the various management views and access requirements overtime.

To help scope and focus establishment efforts for an EA capability increment or EA service enablement undertaking, consider creating a matrix of EA system functions to the EA questions, core EA data concepts and relationships, or EA documentation artefacts that are relevant and required to be automated as a means of quickly detailing the requirements of the system function to be implemented. In Table 20 a simple example is provided for illustration purposes.

Table 20: Example EA System Function Requirements Matrix

Tier	Layer/Thread	Component Type	Component	Component Requirement	Capture Enterprise Component Model	Capture Enterprise Document	Import Enterprise Component Model	Import Reference Model	Classify EA Components by Reference Model	Display Enterprise Component By Reference Model	Display Enterprise Component Views
Business	Products and Services	Service	Duplicate Resource Identification	What current business activities are duplicated across this and other lines of business?						X	
		Entity	BRM					X			

Tier	Layer/Thread	Component Type	Component	Component Requirement	Capture Enterprise Component Model	Capture Enterprise Document	Import Enterprise Component Model	Import Reference Model	Classify EA Components by Reference Model	Display Enterprise Component By Reference Model	Display Enterprise Component Views
	Data and Information		Activity		X						
			Organisation				X				
		Relationship	BRM to Process						X		

Section 5 – The Networks and Infrastructure of the EA function

To link the 'Systems & Applications' level of the EA[3] framework to the 'Networks & Infrastructure' level it is important to focus on what the internal and external hosting requirements are for voice, data, and video networks that the systems and applications create.

Internal (local area network) hosting requirements include application connectivity, the web-based intranet, and all systems that need to connect to the intranet. The use of an Enterprise Service Bus, ERPs, and other middleware solutions to link applications must also be considered.

Due to the organisational and implementation-specific nature of networks, the network details of this layer cannot be readily outlined and therefore no network details are provided as part of the reference architecture. The infrastructure requirements, however, can be outlined in terms of the technical services likely to be required to support the systems and applications outlined in the Systems and Applications layer.

What technical services are the EA function's technology solutions likely to require?

One of the most important and essential tasks of solution architecture within an organisation is to set and use international, national or local - organisational-specific - standards to implement dependent, or realising, technical services where possible. This will help to avoid making the systems and IT environment more complex, reduce costs associated with maintaining the systems and IT environment, and maximise the opportunities for future integration and component reuse. To achieve this requires describing solutions in terms of the technical services that system and application components are dependent on, and/or realised by, and the technical services that the networks and infrastructure components realise or implement.

Based on the type of documentation and data the EA function needs to manage and present, the systems are best classified as standard business support systems requiring common business support system technical services.

Using the US Federal, and Australian derivative, Technical Reference Model to describe the typical types of technical services that an organisation may use or require, in Figure 18 are highlighted an indicative list of technical services the EA function's IT systems and applications are likely to involve. In each of these areas, the enterprise's standard technologies should be identified and reused where possible.

Figure 18 : EA Function Key Technical Service Requirements (Management View)

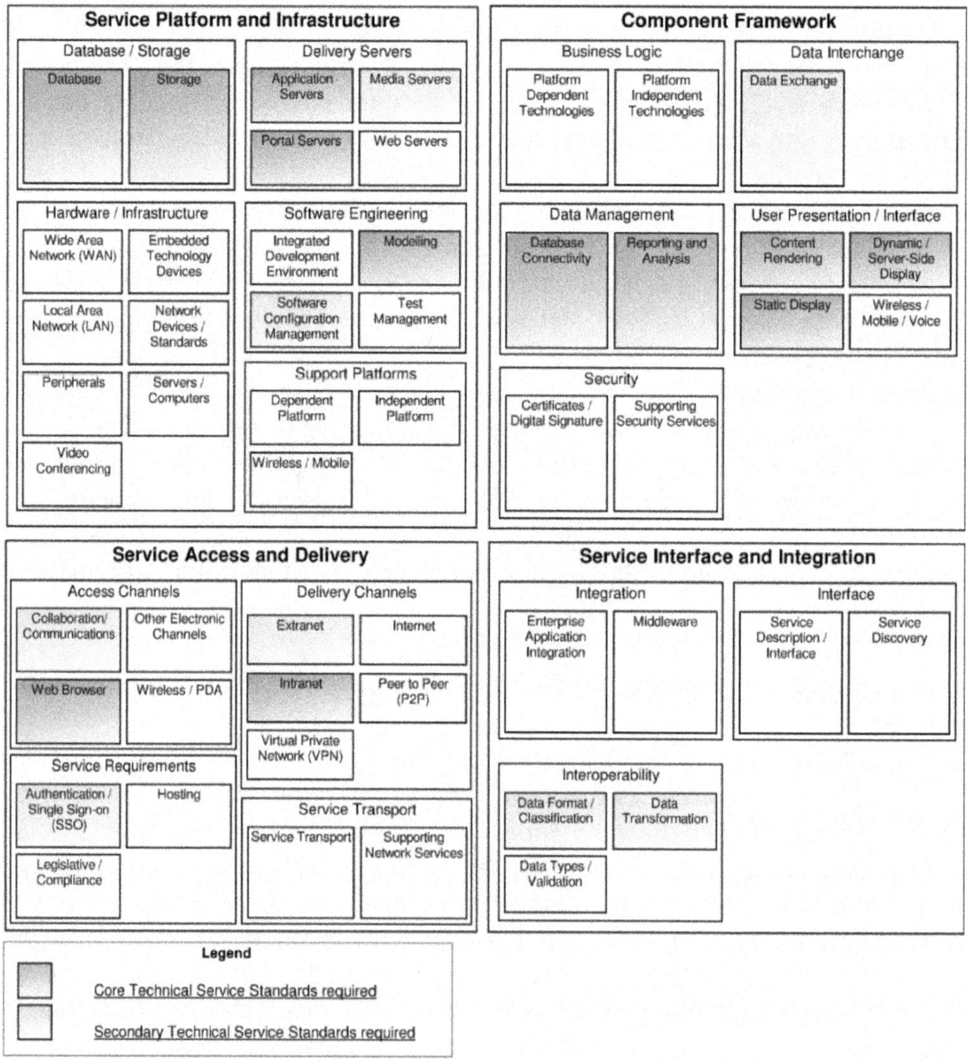

Refer to the Appendix – EA Function Key Technical Service Requirements for a description of each of the highlighted technical services.

What should be considered when documenting and analysing the Networks and Infrastructure Layer?

For An Enterprise

When documenting and assessing the Networks and Infrastructure layer of the enterprise, consider the following:

1. **The Low-Hanging Fruit**

   Planning for and overseeing changes to the networks and infrastructure layer is typically considered the 'low-hanging fruit' of EA. Generally, this layer is under the complete responsibility of the Information Communications and Technology group (or organisational equivalent), with little business input, or requirements, necessary.

   Cost reduction and reduced complexity gains are achieved through rationalising the networks and infrastructure; that is, reducing the variety of operating system types and versions, reducing the number of hardware computer servers, reducing the number of virtual computer servers, standardising on a single database type, providing a single video conferencing solution, etc.

   Analysis of hardware usage and the costs to support and maintain it inevitably turns up many opportunities for networks and hardware simplification, and for application component re-hosting and collocating, with minimal impact and, hopefully, improved system and application performance.

   Also, with the increase in the use of virtualisation of computers, hardware rationalisation as a routine function arises due to the significant simplification of re-hosting applications to new hardware through the elimination of the re-installation and set-up of application components.

   Cloud re-hosting offerings are also increasing the options available when planning simplification and re-hosting initiatives. Cloud introduces new cost models and service levels that were perhaps not previously available or achievable within the organisation given the organisation's legacy environment, current skill sets and available budget. Cloud also opens up opportunities to better align application purpose and importance to hardware location, support levels and the performance characteristics of the networks and infrastructure. For example, retaining in-house hardware and support for all core mission applications due to security concerns while relocating all other applications to a national cloud provider; or retaining in-house all applications residing on Windows operating systems due to deep skills and experience in supporting the platform while relocating Linux hosted applications to a cloud provider.

2. **Reliance on too many vendors versus reliance on too few vendors**

Reduction in vendors is part of the simplification of the networks and infrastructure. Fewer vendors has the following potential benefits:

- o Simpler and better integration between products in the portfolio
- o Greater opportunities to bundle products as part of negotiations
- o Simpler vendor management, due to availability of pre-existing agreement terms and conditions, fewer vendor contacts, etc.
- o Lesser likelihood of large vendors being acquired or going out of business, etc.
- o Greater likelihood of influencing directions or having issues and concerns listened to.

In some instances, however, too few vendors can expose an enterprise to risks such as:

- o Less agility. As fewer opportunities to introduce innovative, high value or better strategically aligned applications into the mix. See the next discussion point for more details
- o Increased vulnerability to security issues. As fewer technology types support a wider range of applications, any security issues in these technologies affects more systems and applications
- o Divergence in business and IT alignment. As vendor's product release cycles and sources of product requirements vary from that of the enterprise.

3. **Network and Infrastructure Rationalisation versus Application Functionality**

As discussed above in the first point of this discussion, reducing network and infrastructure complexity to fewer pieces of hardware and fewer types of hardware and software components can greatly reduce the cost, increase the responsiveness of support and simplify the management of networks and infrastructure.

Achieving this typically means redeploying, re-implementing, re-factoring and/or buying applications that operate within the technology standards profile.

Applications, however, as discussed in the System and Applications section, are the visible and tactile components of systems and applications. Their ability to support service delivery, activity performance and information and data management requirements is where the true value is provided. Also, there are no changes to systems and application that do not result in some degree of change management and/or process reengineering, which is generally underestimated.

So unless the means of achieving networks and infrastructure simplification leaves system and application functionality unchanged, or results in significant performance and/or security improvements to offset any functional changes, benefits may be questionable. For example, narrowing database technology choice so tightly that it prevents or delays a business function from employing a new, innovative system or application that could greatly improve their service delivery is placing too great an importance on networks and infrastructure over strategic and business drivers.

Here is where open standards should help. If open standards were available across all technical services and supported by vendors, in theory an enterprise could operate on a very small set of technology standards across all its systems and application. In reality, open standards and support by vendors for them tends to come in second to competitive differentiation. Therefore, apart from instances in mature technologies or high-profile standards, open standards may not yet exist, may be in their infancy or vary in implementation between vendors, and therefore inhibit the re-use of the enterprise's technology standards.

In summary, be prepared to compromise; define principles that direct toward open standards; focus deployments and bespoke builds on the technology standards profile but be prepared to vary or waiver compliance based on the value proposition of the system or application being evaluated for buy or build. The benefit to the enterprise of having access to a highly non-compliant system or application may greatly out-weigh the costs associated with the increase in the complexity of the networks and infrastructure that would result.

For the EA function

Using the reference architecture to document and assess the EA function's Networks and Infrastructure layer:

1. **Reuse the Enterprises' Technical Service Standards**

   After scoping, prioritising and planning the key strategic, business and system/application components for the EA function, all that remains to do is be a good corporate citizen and, where possible, try and buy or build the required application functionality and employ technologies that reuse the enterprise's technical service standards.

   If a technical service reference model is not already employed within the organisation use the one provided in the reference architecture, otherwise use the enterprises to help identify, where possible, the technologies to be used.

   If the presence or capacity of the available technical services is not suitable to the EA function's technology needs, include in the plan methods to fulfil or realise them that are appropriate to its needs. This may require the EA function to purchase the technologies.

Section 6 – The Standards Thread of the EA Function

One of the more important functions of the EA function is the provision of the standards that are set and used at each level of the EA framework. The EA should draw on accepted international, national, industry and local - organisation-specific - standards in order to promote the use of non-proprietary commercial solutions for EA components. This in turn enhances the integration of EA components, as well as better supporting the switch-out of components when needed. (FUN, EATP).

What standards are unique to the EA function?

Where there is likely to be the most difference between the standards required by other areas of activity within the enterprise and the EA function is in the processes and resources for the delivery and performance of the EA function's core mission services and activities. From an EA^3 perspective, the key areas for which standards need to be set for an EA function are the five key EA elements, i.e.:

1. The method the EA function will follow to document, assess, plan and oversee changes to the enterprise
2. The framework used to scope and communicate the components and linkages that will help to plan and oversee the EA function
3. The standard artefact types that will be used to document and represent the component data and information of the enterprise
4. The tools and repositories that will be used to assist in the consistent management and integration of the documentation and component information
5. The best practices in documentation and analysis that will be used to support the execution and delivery of the EA function's services and activities.

The reference architecture, and the EA^3 approach upon which it is based and documented, by example captures, illustrates and recommends standards in each of these 5 key areas. The reference architecture and its supporting material can therefore be considered the standard for describing and planning the core mission activities of the EA function.

What standards does the EA function share with its enterprise?

For the most part, the standards used and applied to the enterprise at large that are documented and planned by the EA function also apply to the EA function itself. For example, the standards for program and project management, process definition and documentation, technical solutions procurement, development, integration and deployment, etc. for the enterprise should be the same for the EA function.

In the Products and Services and Networks and Infrastructure layers, specific business, enterprise and technical services were identified that the EA function's processes and resources are likely to require or need to help manage and integrate the enterprise's documentation and component information. Against each of these services, the enterprise's standards should be identified and evaluated for appropriateness, readiness and ability to be used by the EA function.

Section 7 – The Workforce Thread of the EA function

The Workforce thread focuses on the organisational requirements associated with the enterprise's future business and technology models.

As part of an EA function, it outlines the key roles and responsibilities, and skills and competencies, of the people required for the governance and execution of the EA function.

Who is responsible, accountable, consulted and informed when undertaking EA activities?

Once processes and resources have been identified within an enterprise it is critical to understand what type of people, or roles, are required to approve their establishment or reengineering, oversee their operations and maintenance and be involved in their performance and use, i.e., their responsibilities.

In Table 21 an overview of the primary roles required to be filled for the effective direction, control and execution of the EA function is provided. They are based on familiar governance, business and IT positions and titles. A detailed breakdown of their responsibilities is then provided in Table 22, described in terms of their participation in various EA activities.

Table 21: EA Function Roles

Role	Overview
Executive Sponsor	Be the champion of the EA program. Provide resources. Assist in resolving high-level EA issues.
Executive Leadership and Decision-Making	Facilitate the establishment and ongoing operation of the EA Program. Lead the resolution of high-level EA issues. Integrate EA and other IT governance processes.

Role	Overview
Chief Architect	Lead the team members, the EA program and documentation process. Undertake EA Program Manager, if required, and EA responsibilities.
EA Program Management	Manage the EA program and documentation processes.
Enterprise Architect	Establish the core elements required to operate and execute the core/mission EA activities. Perform the EA documentation method and management processes.
Requirements Identifier	Participate in EA program decision-making. Promote the identification of IT-related requirements and EA solutions for each LOB.
Requirements Analyst	Document and verify LOB and end-user requirements. Assist in EA component design and documentation activities
Requirements Identification / QA	Identify end-user requirements for EA components. Provide feedback on the effectiveness of solutions.
Technical Analysis and Design	Provide technical analysis and design support for systems-related EA component selection and implementation. Ensure that IT systems meet integration and interoperability requirements. Support EA documentation.
Technical Problem Solver	Collaboratively identify solutions for IT-related problems within LOBs. Support EA documentation.
EA Application and Database Support	Maintenance of EA Software Application. Maintenance of EA repository and information.

The participation classifications that have been used are based on the RACI framework, where RACI stands for:

- Responsible: Those who are assigned the task to carry out the process
- Accountable: Those that have the power to modify the process and are answerable for it success or failure
- Consulted: Those that are involved in the process as a source of knowledge and/or information
- Informed: Those that need to be informed or provided with the outputs from the process.

Table 22: EA Function Role Responsibilities

Role	Participation	Level	EA Activity
Executive Sponsor	Informed	1.1.2	Document and Assess Current Architecture
	Consulted	1.1.3	Document and Review Future Scenarios

Role	Participation	Level	EA Activity
	Consulted	1.1.4	Document Future Architecture
	Accountable	1.1.5	Document the EA Summaries and Sequence Plan
	Accountable	4.1.1	Customer EA Requirements Analysis
	Accountable	4.1.2	EA Documentation Project Scoping
	Accountable	4.1.3	EA Program Reporting
	Accountable	4.1.4	EA Inputs and Output Measures Tracking
	Accountable	4.2	EA Team Management
	Accountable	4.3	EA Maturity Assessment
	Accountable	4.4	EA Communications Plan Creation and Update
	Accountable	3.1.1	EA Framework Selection and Documentation
	Consulted	3.1.2	EA Best Practices Consolidation
	Accountable	3.2.1	EA Tool and Repository Planning
Executive Leadership and Decision-Making	Consulted	1.1.1	Identify and Review Existing Documentation
	Consulted	1.1.2	Document and Assess Current Architecture
	Consulted	1.1.3	Document and Review Future Scenarios
	Consulted	1.1.4	Document Future Architecture
	Consulted	1.1.5	Document the EA Summaries and Sequence Plan
	Informed	1.2.1	EA Reference Model Review and Update
	Informed	1.2.3	Standards Forecasting
	Consulted	3.1.2	EA Best Practices Consolidation
	Consulted	4.1.1	Customer EA Requirements Analysis
	Informed	4.1.2	EA Documentation Project Scoping
	Consulted	4.1.4	EA Inputs and Output Measures Tracking
	Informed	4.1.3	EA Program Reporting
	Consulted	4.3	EA Maturity Assessment
	Informed	4.4	EA Communications Plan Creation and Update
	Informed	4.2	EA Team Management
Chief Architect	Accountable	1.1.1	Identify and Review Existing Documentation
	Accountable	1.1.2	Document and Assess Current Architecture
	Accountable	1.1.3	Document and Review Future Scenarios

Role	Participation	Level	EA Activity
	Accountable	1.1.4	Document Future Architecture
	Accountable	1.1.5	Document the EA Summaries and Sequence Plan
	Accountable	1.2.1	EA Reference Model Review and Update
	Accountable	1.2.2	Standards Identification and Consolidation
	Accountable	1.2.3	Standards Forecasting
	Accountable	2.1	Provide Planning Support
	Accountable	2.2	Provide Resource Management Support
	Accountable	2.3	Assess Business Case Solutions
	Accountable	2.4	Oversee Technology Solution
	Accountable	2.5	Provide Change Support
	Responsible	3.1.1	EA Framework Selection and Documentation
	Accountable	3.1.2	EA Best Practices Consolidation
	Accountable	3.1.3	EA Artefact Guidelines Documentation
	Consulted	3.2.1	EA Tool and Repository Planning
	Accountable	3.2.2	EA Tool and Repository Configuration
	Consulted	3.2.3	EA Tool and Repository Upgrade
	Responsible	4.1.1	Customer EA Requirements Analysis
	Consulted	4.1.2	EA Documentation Project Scoping
	Consulted	4.1.3	EA Program Reporting
	Consulted	4.1.4	EA Inputs and Output Measures Tracking
	Consulted	4.2	EA Team Management
	Consulted	4.3	EA Maturity Assessment
	Consulted	4.4	EA Communications Plan Creation and Update
EA Program Management	Consulted	2.1	Provide Planning Support
	Consulted	2.3	Assess Business Case Solutions
	Responsible	4.1.2	EA Documentation Project Scoping
	Responsible	4.1.4	EA Inputs and Output Measures Tracking
	Responsible	4.1.3	EA Program Reporting
	Responsible	4.1.1	Customer EA Requirements Analysis
	Responsible	4.2	EA Team Management
	Responsible	4.3	EA Maturity Assessment
Enterprise Architect	Responsible	1.1.1	Identify and Review Existing Documentation
	Responsible	1.1.2	Document and Assess Current Architecture
	Responsible	1.1.3	Document and Review Future Scenarios

Role	Participation	Level	EA Activity
	Responsible	1.1.4	Document Future Architecture
	Responsible	1.1.5	Document the EA Summaries and Sequence Plan
	Responsible	1.2.1	EA Reference Model Review and Update
	Responsible	1.2.2	Standards Identification and Consolidation
	Responsible	1.2.3	Standards Forecasting
	Responsible	2.1	Provide Planning Support
	Responsible	2.2	Provide Resource Management Support
	Responsible	2.3	Assess Business Case Solutions
	Responsible	2.4	Oversee Technology Solution
	Responsible	2.5	Provide Change Support
	Responsible	3.1.2	EA Best Practices Consolidation
	Consulted	3.1.1	EA Framework Selection and Documentation
	Responsible	3.1.3	EA Artefact Guidelines Documentation
	Consulted	3.2.1	EA Tool and Repository Planning
	Informed	4.1.1	Customer EA Requirements Analysis
	Informed	4.1.4	EA Inputs and Output Measures Tracking
	Informed	4.1.2	EA Documentation Project Scoping
	Consulted	4.1.3	EA Program Reporting
	Consulted	4.2	EA Team Management
	Informed	4.3	EA Maturity Assessment
	Consulted	4.4	EA Communications Plan Creation and Update
Requirements Identifier	Consulted	1.1.1	Identify and Review Existing Documentation
	Consulted	1.1.3	Document and Review Future Scenarios
	Informed	1.1.4	Document Future Architecture
	Informed	1.2.1	EA Reference Model Review and Update
	Informed	1.2.3	Standards Forecasting
	Informed	4.1.2	EA Documentation Project Scoping
	Informed	4.1.3	EA Program Reporting
	Informed	4.1.4	EA Inputs and Output Measures Tracking
	Informed	4.4	EA Communications Plan Creation and Update

Role	Participation	Level	EA Activity
	Informed	4.3	EA Maturity Assessment
	Informed	4.2	EA Team Management
Requirements Analyst	Consulted	1.1.1	Identify and Review Existing Documentation
	Consulted	1.1.2	Document and Assess Current Architecture
	Informed	1.1.3	Document and Review Future Scenarios
	Consulted	1.1.4	Document Future Architecture
	Informed	1.2.1	EA Reference Model Review and Update
	Consulted	1.2.2	Standards Identification and Consolidation
	Informed	1.2.3	Standards Forecasting
	Consulted	3.1.2	EA Best Practices Consolidation
	Informed	4.1.2	EA Documentation Project Scoping
	Informed	4.4	EA Communications Plan Creation and Update
Requirements Identification / QA	Consulted	1.1.1	Identify and Review Existing Documentation
	Consulted	1.1.2	Document and Assess Current Architecture
	Informed	1.2.1	EA Reference Model Review and Update
	Consulted	1.2.2	Standards Identification and Consolidation
	Informed	4.1.2	EA Documentation Project Scoping
Technical Analysis and Design	Consulted	1.1.2	Document and Assess Current Architecture
	Informed	1.1.4	Document Future Architecture
	Informed	1.2.1	EA Reference Model Review and Update
	Consulted	1.2.2	Standards Identification and Consolidation
	Consulted	3.1.2	EA Best Practices Consolidation
	Informed	4.1.2	EA Documentation Project Scoping
	Informed	4.4	EA Communications Plan Creation and Update
	Consulted	4.2	EA Team Management
Technical Problem Solver	Consulted	1.1.4	Document Future Architecture
	Informed	1.1.5	Document the EA Summaries and Sequence Plan
	Informed	1.2.1	EA Reference Model Review and Update
	Informed	1.2.2	Standards Identification and Consolidation
	Informed	1.2.3	Standards Forecasting
	Consulted	3.1.2	EA Best Practices Consolidation

Role	Participation	Level	EA Activity
	Informed	4.1.2	EA Documentation Project Scoping
	Informed	4.4	EA Communications Plan Creation and Update
	Consulted	4.2	EA Team Management
EA Application and Database SME	Informed	3.1.2	EA Best Practices Consolidation
	Informed	3.1.1	EA Framework Selection and Documentation
	Responsible	3.1.3	EA Artefact Guidelines Documentation
	Consulted	3.2.1	EA Tool and Repository Planning
	Responsible	3.2.2	EA Tool and Repository Configuration
	Responsible	3.2.3	EA Tool and Repository Upgrade
	Informed	4.1.1	Customer EA Requirements Analysis
	Consulted	4.2	EA Team Management
	Informed	4.4	EA Communications Plan Creation and Update

Who are the likely candidates for the EA roles and what skills and experience should they bring to the team?

For each of the roles introduced in the previous section, Table 23 shows the types of knowledge and skills that a person is likely to require in order to play that role effectively. Also against each role is a list of common organisational positions and/or titles that typically fill or that have the right organisational accountabilities and responsibilities, knowledge and skills, to undertake the role.

Table 23: EA Function Roles Competencies and Candidates (Management View)

Role	Competencies	Candidates
Executive Sponsor	Program Sponsorship Leadership Business Management	CEO COO CIO Business Owner
Executive Leadership and Decision-Making	Leadership Business Management	CEO COO CIO Business Owner

Role	Competencies	Candidates
Chief Architect	Leadership Technology Planning C-level People Skills Previous EA Management Plan development	Senior Enterprise Architect IT Strategist
EA Program Management	People Management Program Management C-level People Skills	Chief Architect Programme Manager
Enterprise Architect	Interviewing Workshopping Modelling Presentations Industry	Business Architect Chief Architect Data Architect Solution Architect Systems Architect Networks Architect
Requirements Identifier	Business Planning Business Reengineering	Line of Business Manager Business Planner
Requirements Analyst	Process Review Interviewing Requirements Management	Technology Research Analyst Business Analyst Business Architect
Requirements Identification / QA	Business Analysis Requirements Definition	End-User Representative
Technical Analysis and Design	Technology Strategy Data Modelling System Modelling Network Modelling	Solution Architect Data Architect Systems Architect Networks Architect
Technical Problem Solver	Solution Design Technology Implementation	Solution Architect Systems Architect Networks Architect Technology SME
EA Application and Database SME	Tool Configuration Tool Operations	EA Tools Expert DBA Website Support Web Developer Database Designer Application Developer

Section 8 – The Security Thread of the EA function

Security is most effective when it is an integral part of the EA management program and documentation methodology. A comprehensive IT Security Program has several focal areas including: information, personnel, operations, and facilities. To be effective, security must work across all levels of the EA framework and within all of the EA components. (FUN, EATP)

From an EA function perspective, the types of questions that need to be answered are:

- What standard operating procedures need to be developed to ensure continuity of the EA function operations?
- What design, information assurance, source authentication and access controls need to be put in place around the data and documentation that the EA function documents, analyses and presents?
- What user authentication, security awareness, training and personal identification methods are appropriate to the EA function?
- What physical protection must be deployed to secure the EA systems' operations?

What standard operating procedures need to be developed to ensure continuity of the EA function operations?

The majority of times, an EA function is a management process not a core mission process of the enterprise. Therefore, downtime or unavailability will be tolerated more than core mission processes, and possibly more than most other management processes. As such, no specific disaster recovery and business continuity allowances are likely to be required.

A word of note, however, EA teams tend to be relatively small and transient. The greatest value from EA is also often delivered only in the medium to long term once there's a high degree of standardisation around the data and documentation. In fact, many an EA program or operation has come unstuck due to its reliance on too few individuals to drive and sustain the EA function. Therefore operating procedures that will allow new team members to continue to support the enterprise in a standard and consistent way and discourage the need to 'start again' due to unfamiliarity or unclear procedures is the key requirement of the EA continuity planning.

What design, information assurance, source authentication and access controls need to be put in place around the data and documentation that the EA function manages, analyses and presents?

The information shared with, and managed within, the EA function has the following key security characteristics.

- The majority of the core mission information flows contain data that is **commercial in confidence**. Authorisation and access control is important to ensure access is restricted to only EA customers, whether they are within or external to the enterprise.
- As corporate governance functions are not typically core mission activities, availability of information is not critical. While unavailability of information will be a temporary inconvenience and may result in potential project and governance activity delays, high **availability** is not a mandatory requirement.
- Architecture by its nature aims to support decision-making by focusing on the 'bigger picture'. Ease of communications and decision-making support are of primary importance. An enterprise-wide view of all enterprise components is more important than a detailed specification of individual enterprise components. This often involves abstracting the detail to facilitate understanding, contextualisation and coverage. The **integrity** of the data is therefore likely to be variable in light of the level of abstraction attainable and appropriate to answer EA customers' questions.

  For example, assessing only core or key activities rather than each and every activity; mapping business functions to applications rather than processes to applications; and so on.

What user authentication, security awareness, training and personal identification methods are appropriate to the EA function?

Many people from across the enterprise being supported and represented by the EA function will contribute and consume EA data and documentation. They will either help build, or benefit from, the complete picture of the enterprise in its current and future states and the information about the changes planned to bring about the transition. As such, they will have access to previously hard-to-get-at documentation and data, and more importantly, be able to appreciate and interpret the enterprise and its plans more easily due to the architectural views, linkages and assessments that will be made available.

This improved insight into the enterprise comes with an increase in responsibility to know what can and cannot be done with the information. It therefore becomes necessary to ensure that EA customers are made aware of, and ideally provided with training in, their responsibilities with regards to the use and sharing of EA data, documentation and learnings. For example, the broadening and/or tightening of non-disclosure agreements to include architecture artefacts, or implementing methods and/or services by which EA customers can easily and quickly have validated their requests or needs to share EA data and documentation.

What physical protection must be deployed to secure the EA system's operations?

During the early days of EA function establishment, data and documentation tools and repository solutions are often low tech, poorly funded and/or too small to warrant full IT support. This often results in them being established or deployed on desktop computers or servers outside the enterprise's typical secure and serviced IT infrastructure. Availability and recoverability is therefore subject to the reliability of the computer on which the tools and repositories are installed, and the personnel who knowingly or unwittingly take on the responsibilities of administrator of the software and hardware and custodian of the EA data and documentation. While this may be a necessary condition at this early stage of the EA functions, practices and procedures based on the enterprises' security standards can and should be reviewed and applied where possible, for example, taking regular back-ups and storing them remotely or leveraging the access controls of either the software or tool, if available, or the environment in which the EA system is deployed to prevent unwarranted access.

Section 9 – The EA Program and Transition Plan

A Reference Architecture describes the complete target architecture for an enterprise. A complete architecture can take a long time to implement, more than can be reasonably implemented or established in a single release or project or within the timeframe that initial outcomes are required or expected by EA stakeholders and customers. The environment that an enterprise operates in, the maturity or stage of development of the enterprise and the people that direct, control and execute the enterprise all influence what parts of an enterprise are necessary, required or desired now, and those that can wait.

This is no less true for the EA function. The organisation being served, the maturity of the EA function and the people scoping, managing and performing EA will all in some way influence the schedule and makeup of the EA program and the sequence and scope of the establishment, documentation and analysis activities.

No one transition plan is therefore right for all EA functions. Typically a Reference Architecture does not contain a transition plan. An EA, however, is intended to aid decision-making, in particular in the areas of planning and oversight, by providing not only a current architecture and assessment, and a view of the future or target architecture, but also a plan to transition between the two. As one of the aims of this reference architecture is to provide a realistic example of 'relevant' current and future EA work products, and an EA Management Plan is one of the core mission work products of the EA function, then the reference architecture would not be complete if it did not provide a discussion of the transition and core mission delivery elements of an EA program.

This section addresses the need for an EA program and transition plan, and the fact that no one program or transition plan is right for all organisations, by looking at different capabilities or themes that an organisation might focus on developing depending on its pressing architectural needs or objectives.

As a program of work, as compared to time-specific project, this section covers the planning and execution of the service delivery activities to incrementally and iteratively expand the coverage of the enterprise and the supporting ongoing enablement and operational activities to meet the strategic themes over the long term.

What type of EA capability is required?

Programs of work, or transition plans, for the same enterprise can vary widely depending on its influences and drivers for change. An enterprise facing increasing competition may undertake a program of work, or transition plan, that focuses on research and development of new products and/or services; the same enterprise under threat from uncertain economic times may approve a raft of change initiatives that aim to eliminate inefficient processes and resources; while yet again the same enterprise faced by aging technology hindering organic growth may instigate initiatives that will rationalise, upgrade and refresh its technologies and skills.

From an EA function perspective, the key objectives of its customers and requirements of its core services and stakeholders require that the EA program of work, or transition plan, conduct core and support activities that will develop and execute capabilities that will document, analyse and provide useful information about the enterprise's changeable components. Given the variety of EA customers and services and potential level of maturity and readiness of EA functions five types of EA capabilities, or themes on the above, have been identified. These aim to illustrate how an EA program of work, or transition plan, may be varied to align with its enterprise's needs while still providing good, right and successful EA. The EA capability themes are described below in Table 24, and developed throughout the rest of the section.

Table 24: EA Capability Themes (Artefact)

Theme	Description
Strategic Alignment Planning	Systematic production of EA Management Plans for one or more core/mission areas of the enterprise. Should include practices and activities that are covered in the Standards Enforcement and Redundancy Identification themes.
Cross-Line of Business Service Planning	Strategic or business performance prioritised projects responsible for the production of EA Management Plans for shared business services or enterprise services. Should include practices and activities that are covered in the Standards Enforcement and Redundancy Identification themes.
Redundancy Assessment	Establishment of references models and the discovery, modelling, assessment, reporting and presentation of duplicate

Theme	Description
	and redundant processes and resources for select sub-architecture services and activities.
Standards Enforcement	Establishment of references models and the discovery, modelling, assessment, reporting and presentation of standards for select sub-architecture services and activities.
Component Documentation and Assessment	Component documentation and linkage discovery, modelling, assessment, reporting and presentation to fulfil or answer one or more corporate and/or IT governance function's enterprise information needs and/or questions.

Ideally, but not mandatorily, an EA program or transition plan will include more than one of the themes as part of its implementation. For example, follow up a planning project with one or more documentation and/or assessment projects to ensure the accessibility and usability of the results is adequately catered for.

In Table 25 the customer objectives that are the primary focus of each of the themes have been provided, along with their supporting input and output objectives, to help explain the basis of the themes. These objectives should form the basis of the scoping, and cost and benefit analysis, for all specific EA initiatives, or projects, undertaken.

Table 25: EA Capability Theme Outcomes (Management View)

Capability	Primary Objective	Supporting Objective	Supporting Objective (L2)
Strategic Alignment Planning	Improving effectiveness of planning	EA Management Plans produced	Enterprise-wide architecture components classified
			Emerging trends researched and documented
			Enterprise-wide architecture documented
		Emerging trends researched and documented	Contribution to architecture documentation understood
		Accessible and usable integrated architecture documentation	EA Repository Capability
			Enterprise-wide architecture documented

Capability	Primary Objective	Supporting Objective	Supporting Objective (L2)
		Increased holistic evaluation of resources	EA Management Plans produced
		Technology assessment of all business cases	Contribution to architecture documentation understood
Cross-Line of Business Service Planning	Increased enterprise-wide and LOB planning decisions	EA Management Plans produced	Enterprise- wide architecture components classified
			Emerging trends researched and documented
			Enterprise-wide architecture documented
		Enterprise-wide architecture components classified	EA Modelling Tool
		Enterprise-wide architecture documented	Contribution to architecture documentation understood
		Increased holistic evaluation of resources	EA Management Plans produced
Redundancy Assessment	Increased visualisation of valuable and duplicative processes and resources	Enterprise-wide architecture components classified	EA Modelling Tool
		Standardisation of information on processes and resources	Enterprise-wide architecture documented
			EA best practices and relevant framework adopted
			Standard project management used
Standards Enforcement	Reduced re-work on process and resource	Enterprise-wide architecture components classified	EA Modelling Tool

Capability	Primary Objective	Supporting Objective	Supporting Objective (L2)
	development within programs	Architecture component standards integrated	Contribution to architecture documentation understood
		Technology assessment of all business cases	Contribution to architecture documentation understood
Component Documentation and Assessment	Reduced misunderstandings of resource requirements and potential solutions.	Accessible and usable integrated architecture documentation	EA Repository Capability
			Enterprise-wide architecture documented
		Standardisation of information on processes and resources	Enterprise-wide architecture documented
			EA best practices and relevant framework adopted
			Standard project management used
		EA Repository Capability	

What are the key activities of the capability themes?

In an enterprise, strategic drivers and business performance and priorities will target specific business functions and processes to be introduced or enhanced. From these data and information, system and application priorities can be derived.

On the EA function value chain introduced in Section 2 – The Products and Services of the EA function, for each of the EA capability themes that were identified above, the essential activities - those needing primary effort and focus put into their enablement and execution - and less essential activities - those requiring a secondary degree of attention and effort - that need to be targeted to achieve the theme's objectives are highlighted.

The Strategic Alignment theme-based EA capability key activities

The documentation and assessment of the Strategic Alignment capability projects are focused on supporting the planning decision-making and business-case assessment, allowing the executive level and business managers to decide on a portfolio of work balanced for strategic, business and technology drivers.

While documentation of the current and future architecture is an important part, they are only to be enabled and performed sufficiently to support the production of the summary level documentation of the EA Management Plan, as opposed to populating and publishing the EA repository. As such, the primary and secondary activities for this capability are highlighted in Figure 19.

The EA Documentation Method's activities and outputs for this type of EA capability are the most common to be performed and produced by consulting organisations and equate to the EA development services that they offer.

Figure 19: Strategic Alignment theme-based EA capability key activities (Management View)

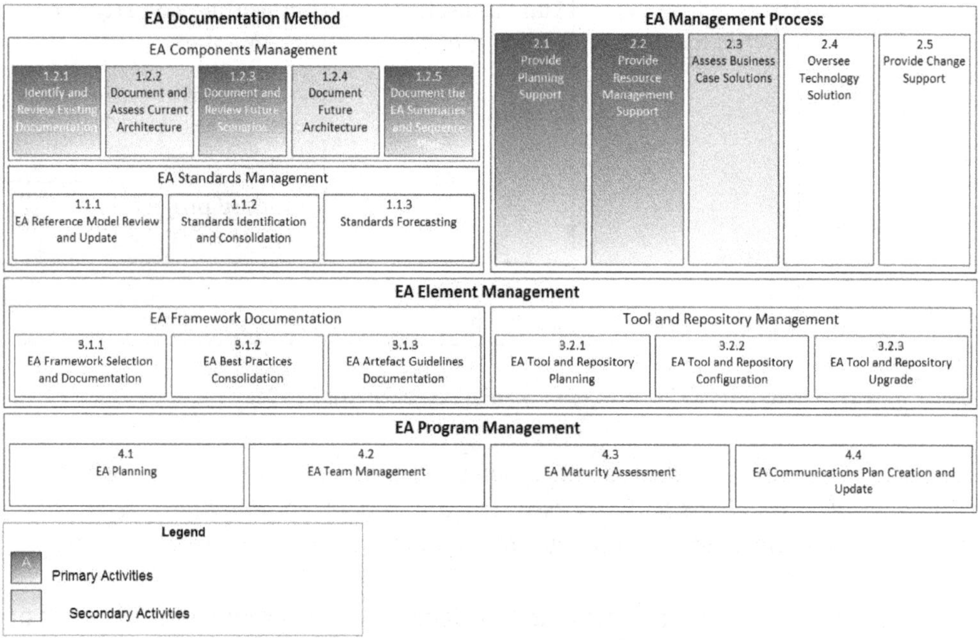

The Cross-Line of Business theme-based EA capability key activities

The documentation and assessment for the Cross-LOB Service capability is similar to the Strategic Alignment-themed project, but focuses on contributing to strategic and resource planning decision-making. This is achieved by allowing enterprises to optimise the establishment and rollout of horizontal business and IT capabilities and services by aligning them to strategic and business drivers and priorities. One example of horizontal business and IT capabilities are the enterprise services in the Service Reference Model, a subset of which is listed in Appendix – Required Business and Enterprise Services highlighting the key horizontal capabilities that contribute to the EA function.

While documentation of the current and future architecture is an important part, they only need be enabled and performed sufficiently to support the production of the summary as opposed to populating and publishing the results via the repository. As such, the primary and secondary activities for this capability are illustrated in Figure 20.

Figure 20: Cross-LOB Service Planning theme-based EA capability key activities (Management View)

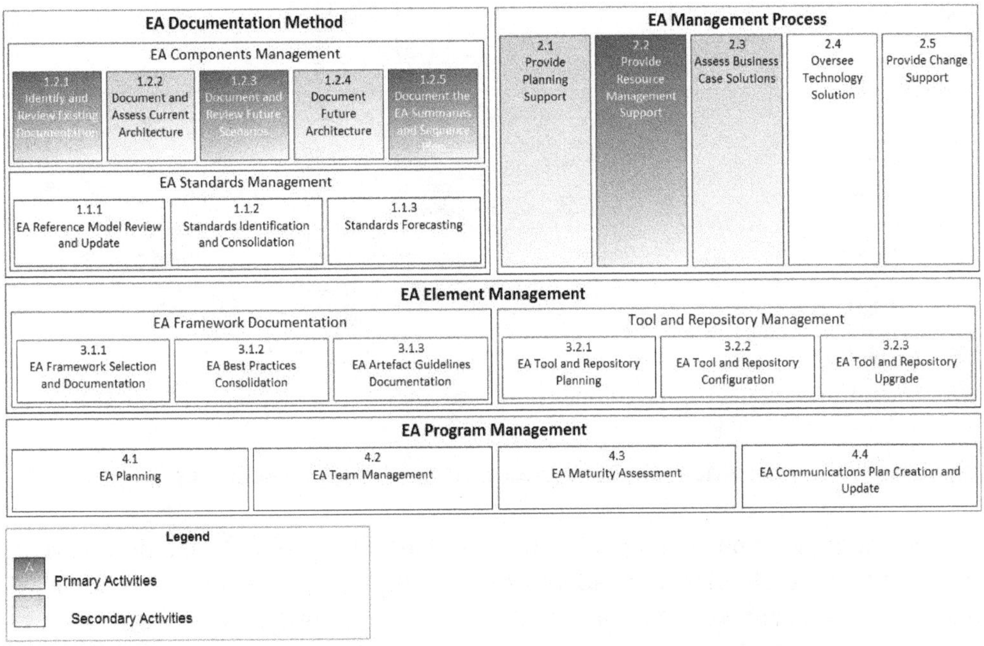

The **Duplicate and Redundancy Assessment theme-based EA capability key activities**

The documentation and assessment for the Duplicate and Redundancy capability is aimed at providing resource managers with the necessary information about the current state of a particular type of process and/or resource that will allow them to align their process and resource rationalisation undertakings with strategic and business drivers and priorities.

Management of reference models that are relevant to the processes and resources that are the subject of the analysis is important to allow clear and concise classification of the enterprise's existing processes and resources, and to highlight and represent overlaps. As such, the primary and secondary activities for this capability are illustrated in Figure 21.

Figure 21: Duplicate and Redundancy Assessment theme-based EA capability key activities (Management View)

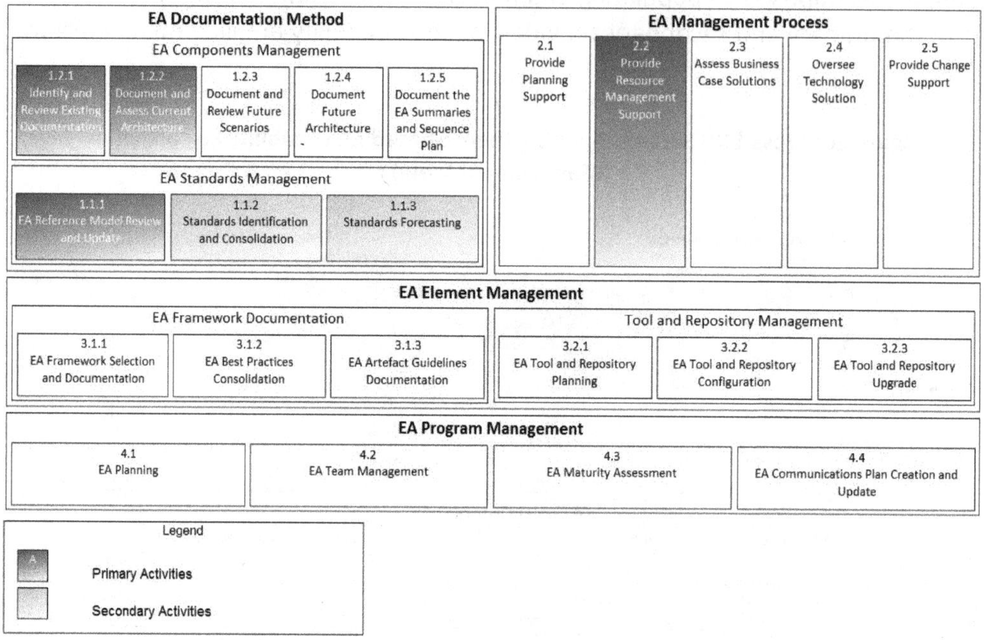

The Standards Enforcement theme-based EA capability core activities

The documentation and assessment of the Standards Enforcement capability aims at overseeing the evaluation and adoption of enterprise standards by technology solutions. Management of the standards set by the enterprise and the reference models to classify them are the primary documentation activities.

Documentation and publication is important in as much as ensuring the standards are easily accessible and that the current implementation of standards for reference purposes is understood. As such, the primary and secondary activities for this capability are illustrated in Figure 22.

Figure 22: Standards Enforcement theme-based EA capability key activities (Management View)

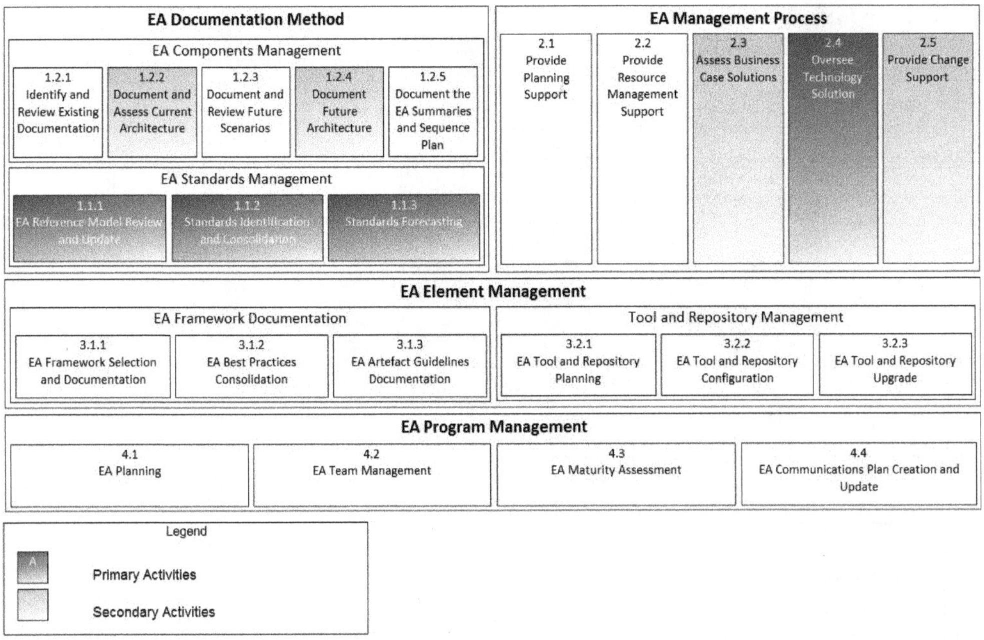

EA Documentation Method				
EA Components Management				
1.2.1 Identify and Review Existing Documentation	1.2.2 Document and Assess Current Architecture	1.2.3 Document and Review Future Scenarios	1.2.4 Document Future Architecture	1.2.5 Document the EA Summaries and Sequence Plan
EA Standards Management				
1.1.1 EA Reference Model Review and Update		1.1.2 Standards Identification and Consolidation		1.1.3 Standards Forecasting

EA Management Process				
2.1 Provide Planning Support	2.2 Provide Resource Management Support	2.3 Assess Business Case Solutions	2.4 Oversee Technology Solution	2.5 Provide Change Support

EA Element Management					
EA Framework Documentation			**Tool and Repository Management**		
3.1.1 EA Framework Selection and Documentation	3.1.2 EA Best Practices Consolidation	3.1.3 EA Artefact Guidelines Documentation	3.2.1 EA Tool and Repository Planning	3.2.2 EA Tool and Repository Configuration	3.2.3 EA Tool and Repository Upgrade

EA Program Management			
4.1 EA Planning	4.2 EA Team Management	4.3 EA Maturity Assessment	4.4 EA Communications Plan Creation and Update

Legend

A — Primary Activities

— Secondary Activities

The Component Documentation and Assessment theme-based EA capability core activities

The documentation and assessment for the Component Documentation and Assessment capability aims at providing a single consistent definition and assessment of components within the enterprise that can be used as a basis for planning and other decision-making activities, whether that be as part of planning, communicating, overseeing or implementing changes to enterprise components.

Documentation and publication of component and component assessment data and documentation in a way that is most useful to the EA customer is more important here than outlining and overseeing adherence to the results of planning activities. As such, the primary and secondary activities for this capability are illustrated in Figure 23.

Figure 23: Component Documentation and Assessment them-based capability key activities (Management View)

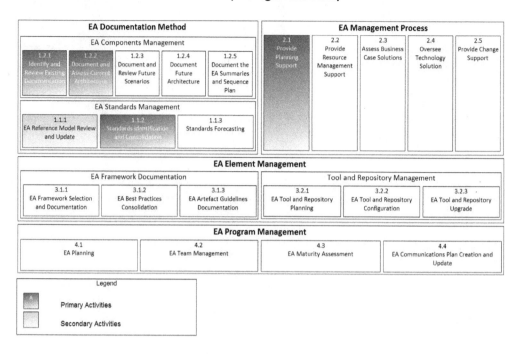

What are the key business and technology components to be established or enhanced?

Over the next few pages are 'storyboards' highlighting the key components across the various architecture layers that are key to the successful enablement and execution of the EA capability themes. On one page the storyboards attempt to help EA planners to determine:

- What the EA function should target its efforts on improving
- What the EA function should aim to deliver to bring about the improvements
- What the EA function needs to do to manage and excel at the delivery of its products and services
- What key information the EA function should source and provide to its activities
- What enterprise components are most required by the EA function to maximise the performance and management of the activities and information
- What automations should be enabled to maximise the performance and management of the activities and information.

The story boards are overlaid on a composite diagram referred to as a 'Horse Blanket', due to their size once all models are placed on the page and rendered at readable size. It provides a view of all the main components of the reference architecture across the layers of the EA framework. A copy of this diagram *sans* storyboard additions is available in the Appendix – EA Function Horse Blanket.

Strategic Alignment and Cross-Line of Business capability themes storyboard

In Figure 24 are highlighted the key objectives and components to be addressed and enabled, respectively, to provide the Strategic Alignment and the Cross-line of Business EA capability themes. In the Appendix - EA Storyboard Details the call outs and key objectives and components are tabulated for clarity.

Figure 24: Strategic Alignment and Cross-Line of Business capability themes storyboard (Management View)

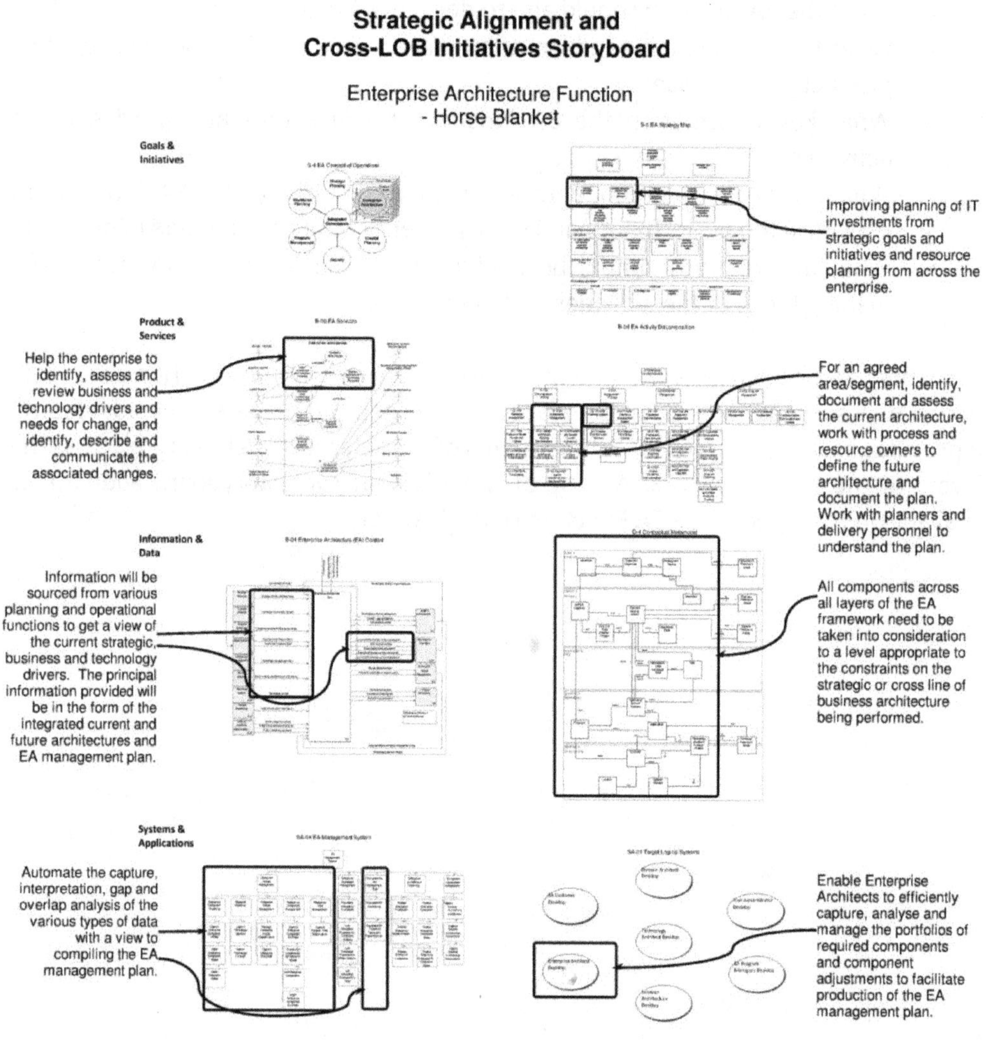

Redundancy Assessment and Standards Enforcement capability themes storyboard

In Figure 25 are highlighted the key objectives and components to be addressed and enabled, respectively, to support the Redundancy Assessment and the Standards Enforcement EA capability themes. In the Appendix - EA Storyboard Details the call outs and key objectives and components are tabulated for clarity.

Figure 25: Redundancy Assessment and Standards Enforcement capability themes storyboard (Management View)

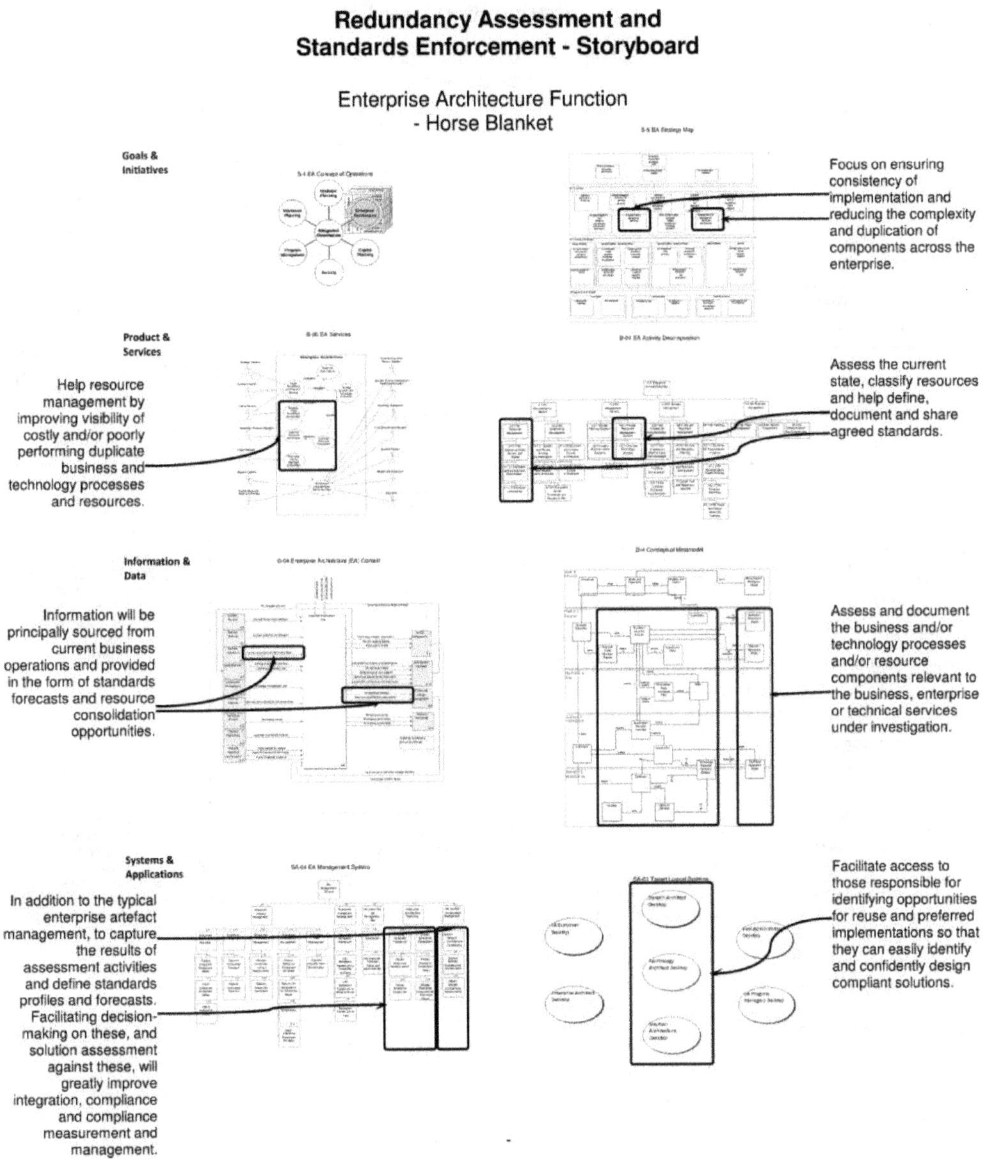

Documentation and Assessment capability theme storyboard

In Figure 26 are highlighted the key objectives and components to be addressed and enabled, respectively, to achieve the EA Documentation and Assessment EA capability theme. In the Appendix - EA Storyboard Details the call outs and key objectives and components are tabulated for clarity.

Figure 26: Documentation and Assessment capability theme storyboard (Management View)

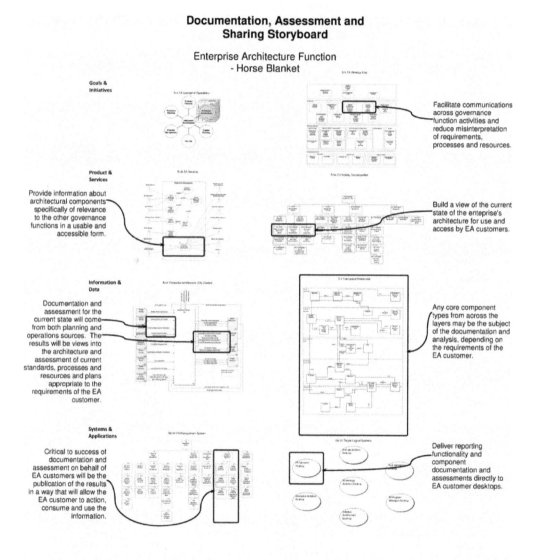

What are the key EA program management and support activities?

Success in the core document method and management process activities is predicated on understanding the requirements and expectations of the EA program and having the right EA function business, data and technology components in place to support them. The key planning and scoping considerations here are to allow sufficient time, budget and resources to enable the EA function to ensure the core EA activities are performed well enough and proportionately to the needs of the enterprise being served.

When planning the EA program and to ensure the EA program has sufficient time, budget and resources to enable the EA function, the EA function manager needs to ensure the:

- **EA customers' requirements and service delivery satisfaction are understood, tracked and being responded to** - Although a significant initial EA program establishment activity, this should be treated as an ongoing activity, repeated at regular fortnightly, monthly or quarterly intervals. For example, regular meetings may be held with key EA stakeholders to understand any new architecture information requirements, the level of satisfaction with existing material, and any changes to strategic and/or tactical business drivers and decisions with architectural impact.

- **EA function's core elements and changeable components are procured, developed and/or enhanced proportionately to the needs of the core EA activities** - This is a significant part of initial EA program establishment that can commence once the type of EA function and services to be established and delivered have been identified. It should be seen as an incremental task rather than a 'one off' task and should be scheduled to occur prior to and overlapping with EA documentation and assessment projects to allow time to ensure new or existing EA function components are enabled as required. For example, tools are available and adequately configured to support the documentation and assessments needed to be performed, artefacts to be created or gathered are well understood, EA customer requirements are clearly understood, and the process, procedures and guidelines for repeating the component documentation and assessment activities are documented.

- **Participants in the EA function's roles are willing and able** - That is, the individuals participating in the ongoing EA activities and/or core documentation and assessment activities are suitably trained and/or recruited.

In Figure 27 an indicative schedule of these business-as-usual activities is provided, illustrating the ongoing nature of the management activities and the regular and recurring nature of the component development and enablement activities in parallel with the ongoing and recurring core EA activities.

Figure 27: Indicative EA Program Management and Support Activity Schedule (Management View)

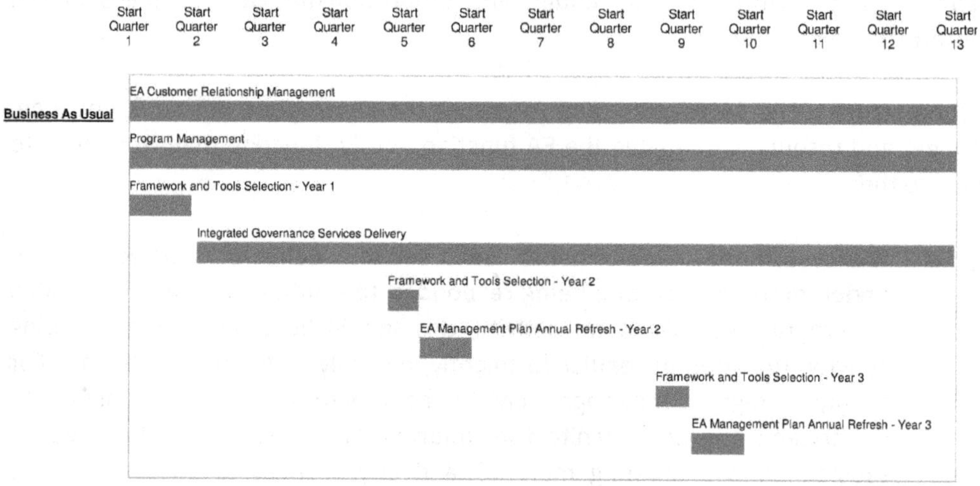

What do the EA program plans look like for capability themes?

Given the competing EA objectives, EA customer requirements and EA resource allocation constraints, a good EA program plan is likely to contain a mix of the following:

- Incremental builds of the architectural documentation, both in terms of enterprise coverage and level of detail
- One-off and recurring EA documentation method and management process activities that will be scheduled as projects and/or tasks
- Ongoing program management, customer management and core element establishment and management activities, to ensure resources address service delivery and housekeeping responsibilities adequately
- Core element establishment and management activities relevant to enabling the primary capabilities of the EA program.

For example, for a Strategic Alignment capability-based EA program, core element establishment and management will be aimed at identifying and supporting the types of documentation and integrated governance service delivery activities that are associated with improving strategy, business and technology alignment and investments.

In the following four sections, indicative program/transition plans for the various strategic capability themes are discussed and illustrated. The plans are described in scenario form, providing realistic examples of the types of projects each theme may undertake, and illustrated in Gantt chart format to highlight the ongoing and recurring nature of integrated governance, EA management and EA enablement activities and one-off and/or time-specific nature of the documentation and assessment activities.

The Strategic Alignment-themed capability EA Program Plan

In Figure 28 an example EA program schedule is provided for a fictitious organisation focusing its EA function on strategic alignment. The EA program consists of several EA Management Plan development projects that will be responsible for incrementally building an enterprise-wide view of how the organisation plans to change to support its strategic directions while delivering support to other governance functions at the earliest opportunity. An incremental and segmented approach was adopted due to resource and time constraints and the need to establish a plan for the first segment as soon as possible.

While this organisation appreciates the importance of a repository and the ease of access EA Management views provide, the emphasis is on the production of the EA Management Plan, and so separate projects are scheduled after each of the management plans are produced, to develop the portal and views into the current and future states and the transition plans.

Figure 28: Strategic Themed EA Program schedule (Management View)

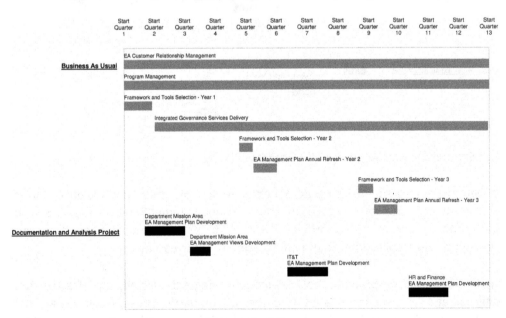

The Cross-Line of Business capability-based EA Program Plan

In Figure 29 an example EA program schedule is provided for a fictitious organisation focusing on improving the support provided to core mission areas by key cross-line of business or horizontal enterprise and business services. Similar to the strategic alignment-based program, individual projects are undertaken over time to allow the EA function to incrementally build the architecture and plans while delivering governance support and information services at the earliest opportunity.

Unlike the earlier organisation, this organisation sees the development of the EA Management Plan and the views of the planned enterprise as equally important, so the results of the planning can be shared and worked from immediately. Each project is therefore responsible for the development of the plan and supporting views of the architecture via the repository/portal solution.

Figure 29: Cross-LOB capability EA Program schedule (Management View)

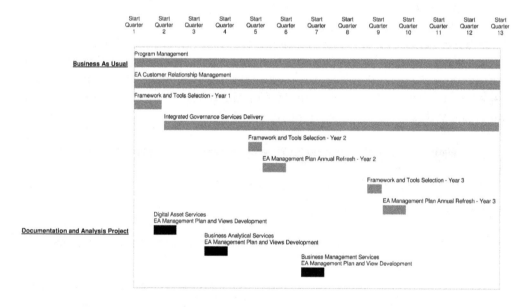

The Standards capability-based EA Program Plan

In Figure 30 an example EA program schedule is provided for a fictitious organisation that wants its EA function to focus on standards management and oversight. Similar to the other plans, individual projects are undertaken over time to allow it to start delivering governance support and information services earlier.

In this organisation, prior to the EA function being established, an infrastructure rationalisation project formulated a number of standards. These, however, are not easily accessible or used during planning, evaluation and implementation activities, and so the first project for the EA function is responsible for the centralisation of the standards information associated with the Services Platform and Infrastructure technical services area and the creation of views that will support usage and decision-making in these service areas.

In the current IT strategy the next areas for rationalisation are the technical services supporting the access and delivery of core mission, business and enterprise services, while there are some standards set and documented, most are missing. A second project is therefore scheduled for the centralisation of existing standards, assessment, evaluation and setting of new standards, and the creation of views for the entire Service Access and Delivery technical service area.

Finally, a business initiative requires a review of the security technical services, so a third project focuses on the assessment, evaluation and setting of new standards and the creation of the Security technical service category.

Figure 30: Standard Identification EA Program schedule (Management View)

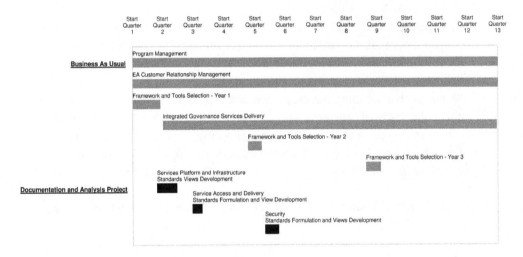

The Component Documentation and Assessment-based EA Program Plan

In Figure 31 an example EA program schedule is provided for a fictitious organisation that wants to improve the visibility, standardisation and accessibility of the enterprise's architecture and assessments. The EA function's role is to facilitate corporate and IT planning by providing views into the organisation of the changeable components, and highlighting key linkages, issues and risks to key stakeholders.

While the component information the EA projects will document and assess will need to be gathered either way to support corporate and IT decision-making, the reason for using the EA function is to ensure that the information is documented in a consistent way, contributes to a repository of information and over time contribute to other stakeholders' activities as well.

In this example program, the organisation starts with no central or agreed repository or portal and plans to undertake several documentation and assessment projects, all adhering to the same EA data model, to ensure that their results can be easily integrated and contribute to the population of a single repository and portal. Each project is focused on different component types and segments that the EA function has agreed with its customers, and is timed to coordinate with planning, evaluation and/or implementation activities that their customers are undertaking. For example, each of the following is being undertaken in governance functions and management processes that are customers of the EA function:

- **To support a line of business planning activity.** The complete set of activities needs to be identified, the issues associated with them agreed and prioritised, and the current planned investment impacts understood.
- **To support a security assessment.** The business mission critical applications and data need to be documented.
- **To support a technical service standards formulation activity.** The current components that directly or indirectly use these technical services need to be identified, and views created to support the planning and assessment of their refresh, replacement or exemption from change.
- **To support a systems development activity.** The current activities using a particular set of systems and applications needs to be agreed and communicated, and any issues associated with these systems and applications made visible. Views to support the use of this information during the planning and change management activities must then be provided.

Figure 31: Documentation and Assessment Program Schedule (Management View)

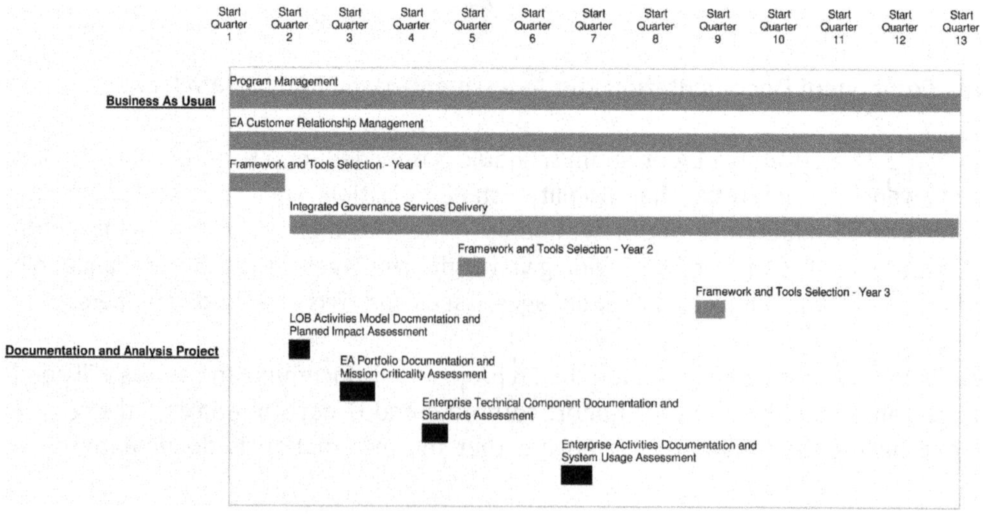

How long are EA capability themed projects likely to take?

The effort associated with EA documentation and assessment projects is dependent on a number of factors and/or dimensions. In Table 26 values for some of the key factors and/or dimensions have been provided to aid, and provide some direction to, the estimation of capability-specific EA documentation and assessment projects. The factors and dimensions include:

- **Segment size** –Is the assessment across one or more multiple organisations, lines of business, business functions, enterprise services, etc.
- **Level of detail** – Are high level abstractions required and relevant given the breadth and short time frame; Is detailed analysis and specification required to reduce the level of uncertainty and increase the accuracy of estimates.
- **Number of layers and/or components** – Does the analysis and documentation require infrastructure coverage given the analysis is focused on business function performance; Are strategic initiatives and goals required given the analysis is on the deployment of applications
- **Thread requirement** – Are security, workforce and standards essential for the current state assessment

The indicative documentation and assessment timeframes include interviews, socialisation and validation with key accountability and contribution stakeholders.

They do not include the time and effort related to the business as usual activities such as customer relationship management and framework and tool selection. The first time a project associated with a particular capability is implemented an additional allowance equal to anywhere between 25% to 75% of the project effort should be included to cover these activities, depending on the availability of existing EA standards within the organisation and how local or international they are. Subsequent projects associated with the same capability should still allow some time for these activities, but somewhat less.

Table 26: EA Capability Themes' project scoping criteria and estimate guide

Capability	Example	Enterprise/ Segment Size	Layers and/or Components	Threads	Level of Detail	Indicative Project Timeframe
Strategic Alignment Planning	Networks Division EA Management Plan	Number of LOBs	All	All	High	13 to 26 Weeks

Capability	Example	Enterprise/ Segment Size	Layers and/or Components	Threads	Level of Detail	Indicative Project Timeframe
	Mobile LOB transition plan Environmental Risk Management IT Strategy					
Cross-Line of Business Service Planning	Customer Management across Mobile and Multimedia LOBs Business Intelligence across all LOBs Data Management across all LOBs	Number of relevant LOBs Number of Enterprise or Business Services	All	All	Medium	8 to 16 Weeks
Redundancy Assessment	Bank Payment processes across all LOBs Agency Geospatial software across all LOBs Utility Access and Delivery service duplication assessment	Number of LOBs Number of Enterprise or Business Services	From Layer in which component belongs, up	All	Medium	4 to 8 weeks
Standards Enforcement	Networks standards Data standards Database standards	Number of Enterprise or Technical Services	Layers in which components for Enterprise and Technical services belong	Standards	Medium - Low	1 to 2 weeks
Component Documentation and Assessment	Process to Application linkages Computers to Application linkages	Number and type of questions about the current or future architecture	Layers in which modelled components belong	As Required.	Medium - Low	2 to 3 weeks per core component combination

Capability	Example	Enterprise/ Segment Size	Layers and/or Components	Threads	Level of Detail	Indicative Project Timeframe
	Data to Activities linkage					

Section 10 – Conclusion and Summary

EA can play an important role in improving the planning, implementation and oversight of the processes and resources, in particular IT ones, of an enterprise - an enterprise being any area of common goal and activity such as one or more business functions, business units or organisations. EA does this by documenting and assessing an enterprise in its current and future state from a strategic, business and technology perspective and developing and overseeing the roadmap or plan that defines how to migrate between the two.

An EA function is the area of common goal and activity, or enterprise, responsible for performing EA within an organisation. As an EA function can be treated just like any other area of common goal and activity, EA can be performed on an EA function to aid its planning, implementation and oversight just like any other enterprise.

A fully functioning, mature and fully resourced EA function based on the EA^3 approach performs a variety of documentation and management activities. It uses and produces documentation and data about the enterprise's business and technology to answer questions, provide direction and insights and clarify agreed and required changes to the enterprise's processes and resources. It provides other business and IT governance functions and management processes with a single, integrated and approved set of information upon which they can collectively manage, change and improve the enterprise.

By applying these documentation and management activities to a fully functioning, mature and fully resourced EA function a reference architecture for enterprise architecture can be developed; a reference architecture against which:

- Real-world EA functions can be measured and compared
- Communications and understanding about EA can be facilitated
- An EA function implementation can be coordinated and planned.

This book has taken this approach and developed such a reference architecture by applying the documentation and management activities of EA^3 to the type of EA function that EA^3 espouses. Ensuring the reference architecture for the EA function draws and builds on the experiences, insights and methods in EA built up over two or more decades.

Appendix – Business Objective to Influence Mappings

In Section 1 – The Goals and Initiatives of the EA function, in response to the question 'What targets should the EA program aim for if it is to deliver a right, good and successful EA function?' a balanced set of objectives was described to address and leverage the influences discussed earlier and to ensure that the EA was good, right and successful. In Table 27 below the principle influences that the objectives sought to address or leverage have been listed to help understand the rationale and expectations of the objectives.

Table 27: EA Objectives to Influences (Management View)

Perspective	Group	Business Objective	SWOT	Influence/Risk
EA Stakeholder		Increasing achievement of strategic goals	Threat	Not Sure If Good Value Is Coming From IT
		Reduced constraints to business performance	Opportunity	Different Answers Given For The Same Questions
			Opportunity	Different Processes Completing The Same Activity with Different Systems
			Threat	Not Sure If Good Value Is Coming From IT
		Technology costs controlled	Opportunity	IT Is Consistently A Bottleneck
			Threat	Not Sure If Good Value Is Coming From IT
			Opportunity	Senior Management Dreads IT Meetings

Perspective	Group	Business Objective	SWOT	Influence/Risk
		Increasing technology support	Opportunity	Different Answers Given For The Same Questions
			Opportunity	Different Processes Completing The Same Activity with Different Systems
			Opportunity	Information For Key Decisions Is Not Available
			Threat	Not Sure If Good Value Is Coming From IT
			Opportunity	Senior Management Dreads IT Meetings
EA Customer		Reduced time to gather and relate strategy, business and technology information	Opportunity	Meeting A New Regulation Is Hard
			Opportunity	Strategic Initiative Is Like Starting From Scratch
		Standardisation of information on processes and resources	Opportunity	Significant Work Activity Around Moving Information From One System To Another
		Increased visualisation of valuable and duplicative processes and resources	Opportunity	Meeting A New Regulation Is Hard
			Opportunity	Strategic Initiative Is Like Starting From Scratch
			Opportunity	Significant Work Activity Around Moving Information From One System To Another
			Opportunity	Senior Management Dreads IT Meetings

Perspective	Group	Business Objective	SWOT	Influence/Risk
		Reduced re-work on process and resource development within programs	Opportunity	IT Is Consistently A Bottleneck
		Increased integration from enterprise-wide planning and utilisation of resources	Opportunity	Significant Work Activity Around Moving Information From One System To Another
		Increased enterprise-wide and LOB planning decisions	Opportunity	Significant Work Activity Around Moving Information From One System To Another
			Weakness	Architecture Scope Is Too Big
		Reduced misunderstandings of resource requirements and potential solutions	Opportunity	Strategic Initiative Is Like Starting From Scratch
			Opportunity	IT Is Consistently A Bottleneck
			Opportunity	Significant Work Activity Around Moving Information From One System To Another
EA Internal Processes	Innovation	Standard project management used	Weakness	Unclear Leadership
			Weakness	Insufficient Resources
			Weakness	Loss Of Key Personnel
	Customer Relationship	EA value scenario and questions understood and prioritised	Weakness	Architecture Scope Is Too Big
			Threat	Lack Of Perceived Value
			Threat	Lack Of Use
		Customer satisfaction tracked	Threat	Not Understanding What EA Is And Is Not

Perspective	Group	Business Objective	SWOT	Influence/Risk
			Threat	Lack Of Perceived Value
			Threat	Lack Of Use
	Operational Excellence - Documentation Method	Enterprise-wide architecture components classified	Opportunity	Meeting A New Regulation Is Hard
		Accessible and usable integrated architecture documentation	Opportunity	Senior Management Dreads IT Meetings
		Architecture component standards integrated	Opportunity	Significant Work Activity Around Moving Information From One System To Another
	Operational Excellence - Management Process	EA Management Plans produced	Opportunity	Strategic Initiative Is Like Starting From Scratch
EA Learning and Growth	Organisation and Culture	Contribution to architecture documentation understood	Weakness	Loss Of Key Personnel
			Strength	Existing Sub-Architecture Skills
			Strength	Existing Sub-Architecture Information
			Strength	Existing IT Governance Functions
		Value proposition of EA understood	Threat	Not Understanding What EA Is And Is Not
			Weakness	Unclear Leadership
			Weakness	Insufficient Resources
			Threat	Lack Of Perceived Value

Perspective	Group	Business Objective	SWOT	Influence/Risk
			Threat	Competition With Other Best Practices
			Weakness	Loss Of Key Personnel
	Information Capital	EA Repository Capability	Weakness	New/Inadequate Technology - EA Tools
		EA Modelling Tool	Weakness	New/Inadequate Technology - EA Tools
	Human Capital	EA certification	Weakness	Loss Of Key Personnel

Appendix – EA Audit Model (EA2M)

In Section 1 – The Goals and Initiatives of the EA function, in the discussion on 'What should be considered when documenting and analysing the Goals and Initiatives Layer?, For the EA function', the use of Dr Bernard's EA Audit Model was raised for the purposes of assessing the current state of the EA function. In Figure 32 is the maturity matrix for the EA Audit Model, EA2M, and a brief description of the audit categories to help explain what they are measuring and why.

The maturity matrix can be used to provide an overview of the key measurement areas of an EA capability. Listed below is a brief description of each of the dimensions and attributes:

- Completeness. The extent and degree of formalisation of the following essential EA elements:
    - Governance or integration of EA with other business and IT planning, oversight and decision-support functions, e.g. Capital Planning, System Development, etc.
    - Methodology or repeatable processes followed to establish, extend, document, use and maintain the EA.
    - Framework or outline of the type and scope of EA data/documentation the EA capability will manage and maintain.
    - Artefacts or EA data/documentation.
    - Tools and Repository or technologies to be used to create, capture, duplicate, access, share, and destroy EA data/documentation.
    - Best practices or methods, approaches, standards adopted by the enterprise to plan, document and implement change, e.g. SOA, BI, BPMN, BPM, etc.
- Consistency, or capability management, in the areas of:
    - Sponsorship and governance of the capability in place.
    - Standards and procedures to follow during the management of the EA.
    - The resources required to allow the ongoing operations of the EA capability.
    - The right knowledge and skills.

Figure 32: Enterprise Architecture Audit Model (EA2M)

	Level 1	Level 2	Level 3	Level 4	Level 5
Enterprise Architecture Audit Model (EA2M)					
Maturity Level	**No Formalized Architecture**	**Foundational Architecture** (General Indicators)	**Extended Architecture** (General Indicators)	**Embedded Architecture** (General Indicators)	**Balanced Architecture** (General Indicators)
Audit Category #1: Completeness					
Governance	Default initial level	EA Governance process selected	Governance initial implementation	Governance full implementation	Ongoing integration with management processes
Methodology		EA Methodology steps selected	Methodology initial implementation	Methodology full implementation	Methodology repeatable and steps optimized
Framework		EA Framework design selected	Framework initial implementation	Framework full implementation	Framework design optimized
Artifacts		EA Artifact set selected	Artifact intial implementation	Artifact full implementation	Artifacts used to support planning/decision-making
Tools / Repository		EA Tools & Repository selected	Tool & Repository initial implementation	Tool & Repository full implementation	Tool use & Repository design optimized
Best Practices		Best Practices selected	Best Practices initial implementation	Best Practices full implementation	Ongoing integration of Best Practices
Audit Category #2: Consistency					
Program	Default initial level	EA program approved	EA program initial implementation	EA program full implementation	EA program optimized
Policy		EA policies selected	EA policy initial implementation	EA policy full implementation	EA policy optimized
Resources		EA resources identified	EA resource requirements met	EA resources fully utilitzed	EA resources optimized
Training		EA training requirements identified	EA training initial implementation	EA training full implementation	EA training optimized
Audit Category #3: Utilization					
Strategic Value	Default initial level	Strategic goals & metrics identified	Strategic goals & business svcs mapped	Strategic goal attainment supported by the EA	Strategic goal attainment optimized via the EA
Business Value		Business services & requirements indentified	Business requirements and IT solutions mapped	Future business service scenarios established	Business services optimized via the EA
Technology Value		Current technology solutions identified	Future technology solutions refined	Future technology scenarios established	Technology use optimized via the EA
Risk & Security Management		Risk & security areas identified	Risk & security solution initial implementation	Risk & security solution full implementation	Risk mitigation optimzed via the EA
Coherency		Coherency goals & metrics identified	Coherency goals initially met	Coherency goals fully met	Coherency optimized via the EA

- Utilisation. The degree of influence and/or use in planning, oversight and decision-making in the following areas:
  - The three management levels of the enterprise - Strategy, Business and Technology.
  - Risk and Security or level of improvement in the number of change and operational issues.
  - Coherency or degree of consistency in definition and description of the enterprise.

Appendix – Architect Documentation and Assessment Service Decomposition

In Section 2 – The Products and Services of the EA function, in response to the question 'What are the types of EA products and services needed to meet EA customer objectives?' a high level description of the EA customers and services was provided. In Figure 33 below the Architecture Documentation and Assessment service has been decomposed to illustrate the principal types of architecture presentation services EA should aim to deliver to each of the key governance functions and management processes EA might integrate with.

Figure 33: Documentation and Assessment Service Decomposition (Artefact B-1)

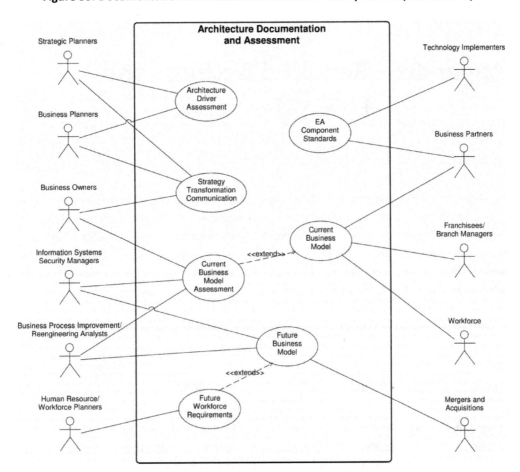

Appendix – Required Business and Enterprise Services

In Section 2 – The Products and Services of the EA function, in response to the question 'What business and/or enterprise services is the EA function likely to require?' an indicative list of services were highlighted on Figure 10, which depicted the US Federal EA (FEA, OMB) Service Reference Model. Listed below are the descriptions of these highlighted business and enterprise services to held understand what they are and why they may be required.

Table 28: EA Function Key Business and Enterprise Service Requirements (Management View)

Service Domain	Service Type	Service Component	Description
Back Office Services	Assets / Materials Management	Asset Cataloguing / Identification	Defines the set of capabilities that support the listing and specification of available assets.
	Human Resources	Benefit Management	Defines the set of capabilities that support the enrolment and participation in an organisation's compensation and benefits programs.
		Career Development and Retention	Defines the set of capabilities that support the monitoring of performance as well as the professional growth, advancement, and retention of an organisation's employees.
Business Analytical Services	Business Intelligence	Balanced Scorecard	Defines the set of capabilities that support the listing and analysing of both positive and negative impacts associated with a decision.
		Decision Support and Planning	Defines the set of capabilities that support the analysis of information and

Service Domain	Service Type	Service Component	Description
			predict the impact of decisions before they are made.
	Reporting	Ad hoc	Defines the set of capabilities that support the use of dynamic reports on an as needed basis.
		OLAP	Defines the set of capabilities that support the analysis of information that has been summarised into multidimensional views and hierarchies.
	Visualisation	Graphing / Charting	Defines the set of capabilities that support the presentation of information in the form of diagrams or tables.
	Knowledge Discovery	Data Mining	Defines the set of capabilities that support the efficient discovery of non-obvious, valuable patterns and relationships within a large collection of data.
		Modelling	Defines the set of capabilities that support the development of descriptions to adequately explain relevant data for the purpose of prediction, pattern detection, exploration or general organisation of data.
		Simulation	Defines the set of capabilities that support the utilisation of models to mimic real-world processes, paper forms.
Business Management Services	Investment Management	Performance Management	Defines the set of capabilities for measuring the effectiveness of an organisation's financial assets and capital.
		Portfolio Management	Defines the set of capabilities that support the administration of a group of investments held by an organisation.

Service Domain	Service Type	Service Component	Description
		Strategic Planning and Mgmt	Defines the set of capabilities that support the determination of long-term goals and the identification of the best approach for achieving those goals.
	Management of Process	Change Management	Defines the set of capabilities that control the process for updates or modifications to the existing documents, software or business processes of an organisation.
		Program / Project Management	Defines the set of capabilities for the management and control of a particular effort of an organisation.
		Requirements Management	Defines the set of capabilities for gathering, analysing and fulfilling the needs and prerequisites of an organisation's efforts.
		Risk Management	Defines the set of capabilities that support the identification and probabilities or chances of hazards as they relate to a task, decision or long-term goal; includes risk assessment and risk mitigation.
	Organisational Management	Network Management	Defines the set of capabilities involved in monitoring and maintaining a communications network in order to diagnose problems, gather statistics and provide general usage.
Customer Services	Customer-Initiated Assistance	Scheduling	Defines the set of capabilities that support the plan for performing work or services to meet the needs of an organisation's customers.
	Customer Relationship Management	Customer Analytics	Defines the set of capabilities that allow for the analysis of an organisation's customers as well as the scoring of third party information as it relates to an organisation's customers.
		Customer Feedback	Defines the set of capabilities that are used to collect, analyse and handle

Service Domain	Service Type	Service Component	Description
			comments and feedback from an organisation's customers.
		Surveys	Defines the set of capabilities that are used to collect useful information from an organisation's customers.
Digital Asset Services	Document Management	Document Conversion	Defines the set of capabilities that support the changing of files from one type of format to another.
		Document Referencing	Defines the set of capabilities that support the redirection to other documents and information for related content.
		Document Review and Approval	Defines the set of capabilities that support the editing and commendation of documents before releasing them.
		Document Revisions	Defines the set of capabilities that support the versioning and editing of content and documents.
	Knowledge Management	Information Retrieval	Defines the set of capabilities that allow access to data and information for use by an organisation and its stakeholders.
		Information Sharing	Defines the set of capabilities that support the use of documents and data in a multi-user environment for use by an organisation and its stakeholders.
		Knowledge Capture	Defines the set of capabilities that facilitate collection of data and information.
		Knowledge Distribution and Delivery	Defines the set of capabilities that support the transfer of knowledge to the end user.
		Knowledge Engineering	Defines the set of capabilities that support the translation of knowledge from an expert into the knowledge base of an expert system.
	Records Management	Digital Rights Management	Defines the set of capabilities that support the claim and ownership of

Service Domain	Service Type	Service Component	Description
			intellectual capital and artefacts belonging to an organisation.
		Document Classification	Defines the set of capabilities that support the categorisation of documents and artefacts, both electronic and physical.
Support Services	Collaboration	Document Library	Defines the set of capabilities that support the grouping and archiving of files and records on a server.
	Communication	Computer / Telephony Integration	Defines the set of capabilities that support the connectivity between server hardware, software and telecommunications equipment into a single logical system.
	Forms Management	Forms Creation	Defines the set of capabilities that support the design and generation of electronic or physical forms and templates for use within the business cycle by an organisation and its stakeholders.
		Forms Modification	Defines the set of capabilities that support the maintenance of electronic or physical forms, templates and their respective elements and fields.
	Search	Classification	Defines the set of capabilities that support selection and retrieval of records organised by shared characteristics in content or context.
		Query	Defines the set of capabilities that support retrieval of records that satisfy specific query selection criteria.
	Security Management	Access Control	Defines the set of capabilities that support the management of permissions for logging onto a computer, application, service or network; includes user management and role/privilege management.

Service Domain	Service Type	Service Component	Description
		Audit Trail Capture and Analysis	Defines the set of capabilities that support the identification and monitoring of activities within an application, system or network.
	Systems Management	License Management	Defines the set of capabilities that support the purchase, upgrade and tracking of legal usage contracts for system software and applications.
		Software Distribution	Defines the set of capabilities that support the propagation, installation and upgrade of written computer programs, applications and components.
Back Office Services	Assets / Materials Management	Asset Cataloguing / Identification	Defines the set of capabilities that support the listing and specification of available assets.
	Human Resources	Benefit Management	Defines the set of capabilities that support the enrolment and participation in an organisation's compensation and benefits programs.
		Career Development and Retention	Defines the set of capabilities that support the monitoring of performance as well as the professional growth, advancement, and retention of an organisation's employees.

Appendix – Business and Enterprise Service Components by Dependent EA Activity

To help prioritise the assessment of the business and enterprise services for use by, and to support, the EA function, listed below are the key services components from the previous section grouped by the key leaf level EA activities with the need of the service.

Table 29: Key Business and Enterprise Service Components by Activity (Management View)

#	EA Activity	Service Domain	Service Type	Service Components
1.1.1	Identify and Review Existing Documentation	Business Analytical Services	Reporting	Ad hoc
		Digital Asset Services	Records Management	Digital Rights Management
		Digital Asset Services	Records Management	Document Classification
		Support Services	Collaboration	Document Library
		Digital Asset Services	Knowledge Management	Knowledge Capture
1.1.2	Document and Assess Current Architecture	Business Analytical Services	Reporting	Ad hoc
		Back Office Services	Assets / Materials Management	Asset Cataloguing / Identification
		Support Services	Security Management	Audit Trail Capture and Analysis
		Business Analytical Services	Business Intelligence	Balanced Scorecard
		Support Services	Search	Classification

#	EA Activity	Service Domain	Service Type	Service Components
		Support Services	Communication	Computer / Telephony Integration
		Business Analytical Services	Business Intelligence	Decision Support and Planning
		Digital Asset Services	Document Management	Document Conversion
		Support Services	Collaboration	Document Library
		Digital Asset Services	Document Management	Document Referencing
		Digital Asset Services	Document Management	Document Review and Approval
		Business Analytical Services	Visualisation	Graphing / Charting
		Digital Asset Services	Knowledge Management	Information Sharing
		Digital Asset Services	Knowledge Management	Knowledge Capture
		Business Analytical Services	Knowledge Discovery	Modelling
		Business Analytical Services	Reporting	OLAP
		Support Services	Search	Query
1.1.3	Document and Review Future Scenarios	Support Services	Communication	Computer / Telephony Integration
		Digital Asset Services	Document Management	Document Referencing
		Digital Asset Services	Document Management	Document Review and Approval
		Digital Asset Services	Knowledge Management	Information Sharing
		Digital Asset Services	Knowledge Management	Knowledge Engineering

#	EA Activity	Service Domain	Service Type	Service Components
1.1.4	Document Future Architecture	Support Services	Security Management	Audit Trail Capture and Analysis
		Support Services	Search	Classification
		Support Services	Communication	Computer / Telephony Integration
		Digital Asset Services	Document Management	Document Review and Approval
		Business Analytical Services	Visualisation	Graphing / Charting
		Digital Asset Services	Knowledge Management	Information Sharing
		Digital Asset Services	Knowledge Management	Knowledge Engineering
		Business Analytical Services	Knowledge Discovery	Modelling
		Business Analytical Services	Reporting	OLAP
1.1.5	Document the EA Summaries and Sequence Plan	Support Services	Communication	Computer / Telephony Integration
		Digital Asset Services	Document Management	Document Review and Approval
		Digital Asset Services	Document Management	Document Revisions
		Business Analytical Services	Visualisation	Graphing / Charting
		Digital Asset Services	Knowledge Management	Information Sharing
		Digital Asset Services	Knowledge Management	Knowledge Engineering
		Business Analytical Services	Knowledge Discovery	Modelling
		Business Analytical Services	Reporting	OLAP

#	EA Activity	Service Domain	Service Type	Service Components
2.1	Provide Planning Support	Business Analytical Services	Reporting	Ad hoc
		Support Services	Communication	Computer / Telephony Integration
		Business Analytical Services	Knowledge Discovery	Data Mining
		Business Analytical Services	Business Intelligence	Decision Support and Planning
		Digital Asset Services	Knowledge Management	Knowledge Distribution and Delivery
		Support Services	Search	Query
2.2	Provide Resource Management Support	Support Services	Communication	Computer / Telephony Integration
		Business Analytical Services	Business Intelligence	Decision Support and Planning
		Digital Asset Services	Knowledge Management	Knowledge Distribution and Delivery
		Support Services	Search	Query
2.3	Assess Business Case Solutions	Support Services	Communication	Computer / Telephony Integration
		Digital Asset Services	Knowledge Management	Knowledge Distribution and Delivery
		Support Services	Search	Query
2.4	Oversee Technology Solution	Support Services	Communication	Computer / Telephony Integration
		Digital Asset Services	Knowledge Management	Knowledge Distribution and Delivery

#	EA Activity	Service Domain	Service Type	Service Components
2.5	Provide Change Support	Support Services	Communication	Computer / Telephony Integration
		Digital Asset Services	Knowledge Management	Knowledge Distribution and Delivery
		Support Services	Search	Query
3.1.1	EA Framework Selection and Documentation	Digital Asset Services	Records Management	Document Classification
		Support Services	Collaboration	Document Library
		Digital Asset Services	Document Management	Document Referencing
		Digital Asset Services	Document Management	Document Revisions
		Digital Asset Services	Knowledge Management	Knowledge Capture
3.1.2	EA Best Practices Consolidation	Digital Asset Services	Records Management	Document Classification
		Support Services	Collaboration	Document Library
		Digital Asset Services	Document Management	Document Referencing
		Digital Asset Services	Document Management	Document Revisions
		Digital Asset Services	Knowledge Management	Knowledge Capture
3.1.3	EA Artefact Guidelines Documentation	Digital Asset Services	Records Management	Document Classification
		Support Services	Collaboration	Document Library
		Digital Asset Services	Document Management	Document Referencing
		Digital Asset Services	Document Management	Document Revisions
		Digital Asset Services	Knowledge Management	Knowledge Capture

#	EA Activity	Service Domain	Service Type	Service Components
3.2.2	EA Tool and Repository Configuration	Support Services	Security Management	Access Control
		Support Services	Forms Management	Forms Creation
		Support Services	Forms Management	Forms Modification
3.2.3	EA Tool and Repository Upgrade	Support Services	Systems Management	License Management
		Support Services	Systems Management	Software Distribution
4.1.1	Customer EA Requirements Analysis	Customer Services	Customer Relationship Management	Customer Analytics
		Customer Services	Customer Relationship Management	Customer Feedback
		Customer Services	Customer Relationship Management	Surveys
4.1.2	EA Documentation Project Scoping	Customer Services	Customer-Initiated Assistance	Scheduling
4.2	EA Team Management	Back Office Services	Human Resources	Career Development and Retention

Appendix – The Activity Information Flow Decomposition

In Section 3 – The Data and Information of the EA function, in response to the question, 'What types of information flows are required to support the EA function's service delivery and operations responsibilities?', on page 92, a context diagram outlining the major input and output information flows to EA was provided and discussed.

In this appendix the EA function is decomposed to illustrate the information input and output responsibilities of the various child EA activities in support of the function's service delivery and operational responsibilities.

The Level A0 – Enterprise Architecture Activity Flow

Figure 34: Level A0 - Enterprise Architecture activity flow (Artefact D-2)

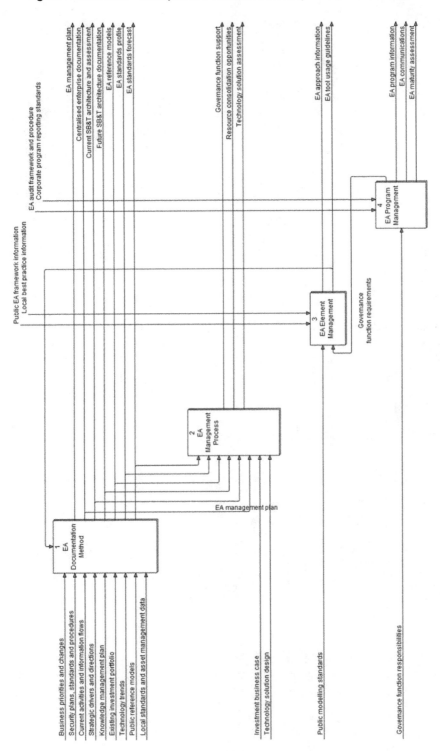

The Level A1 – EA Documentation Method

Figure 35: Level A1 – EA Documentation Method activity flow (Artefact D-2)

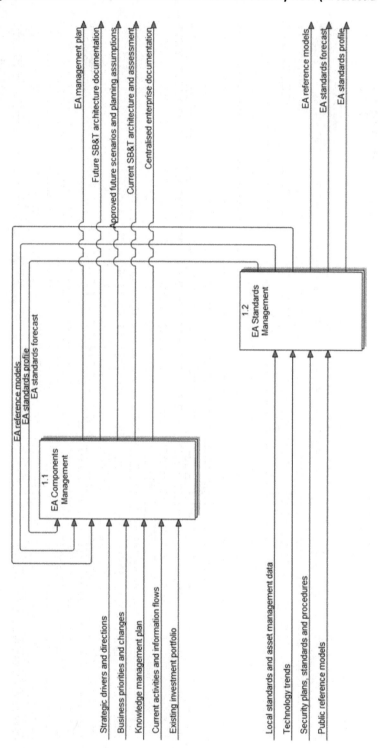

The Level A1.1 – EA Component Management

Figure 36: Level A1.1 - EA Component Management activity flow (Artefact D-2)

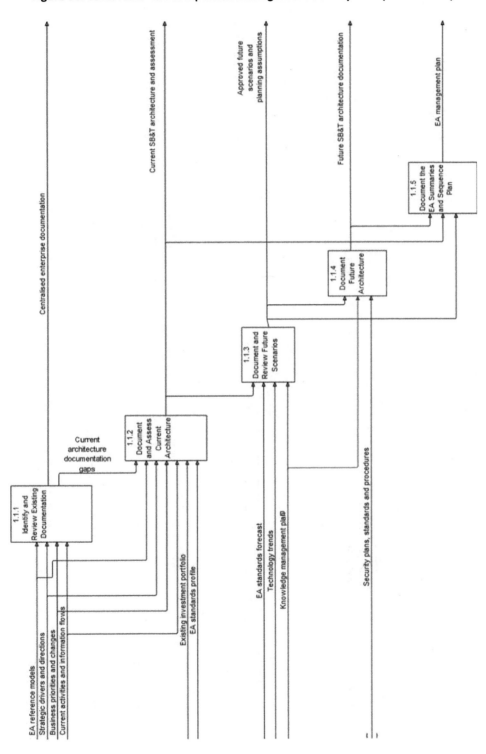

The Level A1.2 – EA Standards Management

Figure 37: Level A1.2 - EA Standards Management activity flow (Artefact D-2)

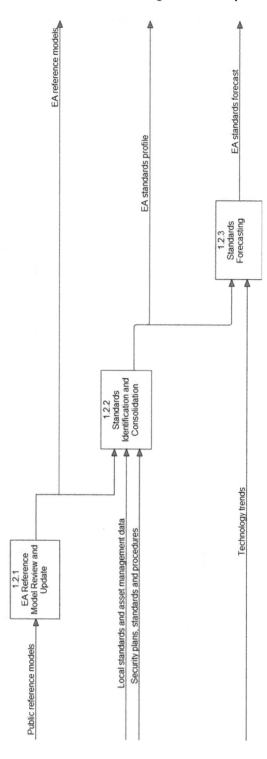

The Level A2 – EA Management Process

Figure 38: Level A3 – EA Management Process activity flow (Artefact D-2)

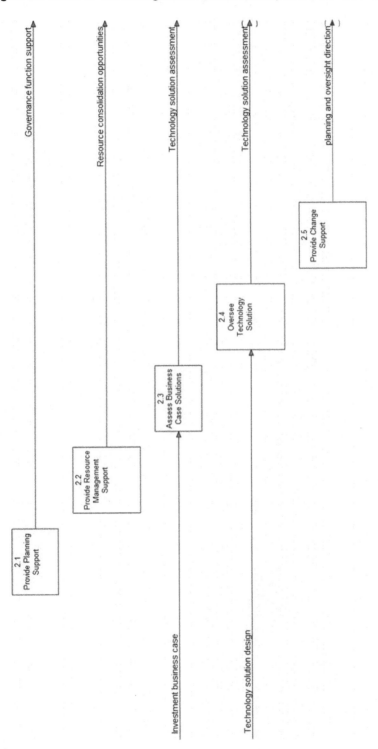

The Level A3 – EA Element Management

Figure 39: Level A3 - EA Element Management information flows (Artefact D-2)

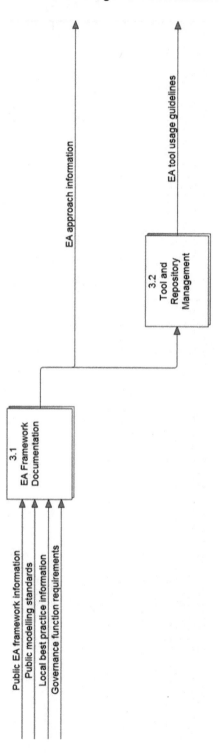

The Level A4 – EA Program Management

Figure 40: Level A4 - EA Program Management activity flow (Artefact D-2)

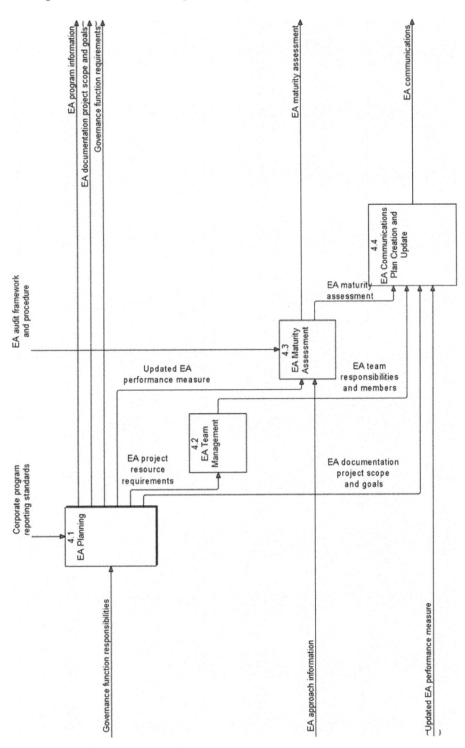

The Level A4.1 – EA Planning

Figure 41: Level A4 - EA Planning activity flow (Artefact D-2)

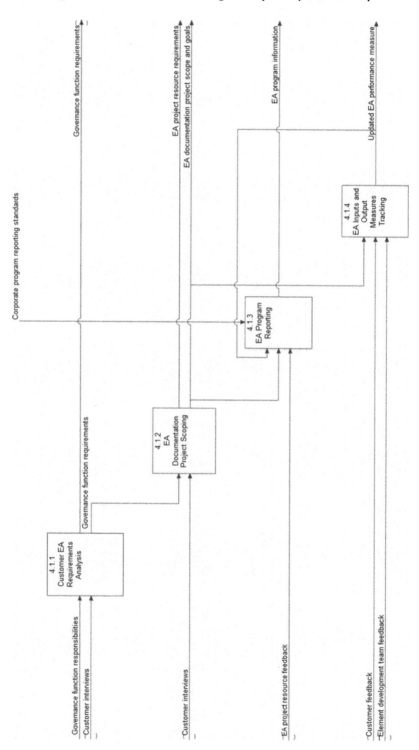

Appendix – Principal EA Information Flow Descriptions

In Section 3 – The Data and Information of the EA function, in response to the question, 'What types of information flows are required to support the EA function's service delivery and operations responsibilities?', on page 92, a context diagram outlining the major input and output information flows to EA was provided and discussed. Listed below are the descriptions for each of these.

Of note is that it describes the information needs and outputs from the EA function without thought to the structure, format, etc. to highlight the type of knowledge transfer requirement necessary, as opposed to how the knowledge is being transferred.

Table 30: Principal EA Information Flows (Artefact D-2)

Information Exchange	Description		Function
Business priorities and changes	The future plans for the line of business including the organisational structure changes, new and improved business functions/activities/processes, new and changed information requirements and an idea of the funding requirements and budgets.	From	Business Planning
		To	Enterprise Architecture (EA)
Centralised enterprise documentation	Readily accessible copies of the reference information upon which the EA assessments, analysis and management plans are based.	From	Enterprise Architecture (EA)
		To	Planning and Oversight
Corporate program reporting standards	The way in which programs are meant to be reported to ensure the portfolio and individual investments can be managed effectively and transparently.	To	Enterprise Architecture (EA)

Information Exchange	Description		Function
Current SBT architecture and assessment	The integrated set of artefacts, documents and data that provides an overview of the current state of the enterprise's components, their key interdependencies and details of the gaps in their performance, capability to deliver on the strategies and sustainability.	From	Enterprise Architecture (EA)
		To	Planning and Oversight
Current activities and information flows	The activities that the business currently performs, including details of the organisational and performance issues impacting execution, and the documentation and data that they use and share while undertaking the activities.	From	Business Operations
		To	Enterprise Architecture (EA)
EA audit framework and procedure	The method to be used to continually assess the maturity and progress of the EA function and assist the planning and improvement of the EA function.	To	Enterprise Architecture (EA)
EA communications	The EA program overview, including its purpose, plan, approach and benefits, plus answers to commonly-asked questions about the practice of EA that will facilitate the engagement and support of EA services.	From	Enterprise Architecture (EA)
		To	Program Monitoring
EA management plan	Information about the enterprise's strategic goals and initiatives, performance gaps and resource requirements, planned solutions and sequencing/transition plan, and a summary of the current and future architectures.	From	Enterprise Architecture (EA)
		To	Capital Planning
EA maturity assessment	The results of an EA maturity assessment identifying the strengths and weaknesses of the EA program, any risks or issues, the priorities for improvements to the program plan, and the rating and realistic benchmarking.	From	Enterprise Architecture (EA)
		To	Program Monitoring
EA program information	The EA program reporting information outlining progress to plan, for example, actual vs. forecast spend, issues and risks, and successes and outputs.	From	Enterprise Architecture (EA)
		To	Program Monitoring

Information Exchange	Description		Function
EA reference models	The enterprise strategy, business and technology models and taxonomies used to provide an agreed enterprise-wide description of the enterprise, and to classify the components in each layer of the architecture to aid communications, gap and overlap analysis, and change focus.	From	Enterprise Architecture (EA)
		To	Planning and Oversight
EA standards forecast	The internal and external emerging trends and market realities in each of the service component and technical services areas that need to be considered when planning changes, as they may represent opportunities for improvements or threats to the current architecture.	From	Enterprise Architecture (EA)
		To	IT Lifecycle/Change Management
EA standards profile	The current standards, products and specifications in each of the service component and technical service areas that the enterprise has agreed on to help facilitate improved information sharing and IT service delivery.	From	Enterprise Architecture (EA)
		To	System Development
EA tool usage guidelines	The set-up, access and use principles and standards for the tools and repository that will facilitate the accurate, secure and useful modelling and documentation of the enterprise's architecture for EA purposes.	From	Enterprise Architecture (EA)
		To	System Development
Existing investment portfolio	The existing investments planned or scheduled to be worked on by the organisation to change the enterprise components. These may have arisen through alternative planning activities or resulted from change request and tactical initiatives.	From	Capital Planning
		To	Enterprise Architecture (EA)
Future SBnT architecture documentation	The integrated set of artefacts that describe the future strategies, business model and supporting technology solutions targeted by the plan.	From	Enterprise Architecture (EA)
		To	Planning and Oversight
	An overview of the planning and oversight responsibilities of the governance function.	From	Planning and Oversight

Information Exchange	Description		Function
Governance function responsibilities		To	Enterprise Architecture (EA)
Governance function support	Provision of information about the enterprise in its current or future state and the plans to transition between the two that allow the corporate and IT planning and oversight to be performed with improved confidence and certainty.	From	Enterprise Architecture (EA)
		To	Planning and Oversight
Investment business case	An overview and rationale for the changes intended to be made to the enterprise including value, benefit or achievement against objectives brought about by the investment, the issues that will hinder success, and risk a return on investments made in technology and other resources.	From	Capital Planning
		To	Enterprise Architecture (EA)
Knowledge management plan	A description of the way in which the enterprise will gather, organise, share and analyse its knowledge in terms of data and information, as well as resources, capabilities and activities, to promote the seamless provision and presentation of data and information from multiple sources.	From	Information Management
		To	Enterprise Architecture (EA)
Local best practice information	Existing best practices used within the enterprise to plan changes to its enterprise components to address strategic, performance and asset-related drivers, for example, ITIL, Business Reengineering and PMI.	From	Practice Engineering
		To	Enterprise Architecture (EA)
Local standards and asset management data	The standards and asset plans for the various service components and technical services maintained across the enterprise to help the consistent change and improvement of the enterprise.	From	IT Lifecycle/Change Management
		To	Enterprise Architecture (EA)
Public EA framework information	The literature, including papers, books, reviews, etc. about the adoption and use of public and/or industry EA frameworks.	From	Industry Standards Determination

Information Exchange	Description		Function
		To	Enterprise Architecture (EA)
Public modelling standards	The literature, including papers, books, reviews, etc.about standards or commonly accepted methods of modelling enterprise components.	From	Industry Standards Determination
		To	Enterprise Architecture (EA)
Public reference models	The architecture models, taxonomies and classification schemes that provide a complete and enterprise-wide description of various types of EA components, typically based on best practices and experience. For example, the FEA BRM, SRM and TRM, TOGAF TRM and eTOM Context Model. They are typically used to standardise terminology, and identification and communication of gaps and overlaps in the current architecture, and represent an ideal and complete target.	From	Industry Standards Determination
		To	Enterprise Architecture (EA)
Resource consolidation opportunities	The potential business and technology enterprise components that are candidates for consolidation, standardisation and rationalisation or horizontalisation and reuse based on such things as supporting the strategic directions, existing capability assessment and cost profile.	From	Enterprise Architecture (EA)
		To	IT Lifecycle/Change Management
Security plans, standards and procedures	The current and planned standards and procedures to be followed or implemented to reduce the risk of security-related incidents.	From	Security Planning
		To	Enterprise Architecture (EA)
Strategic drivers and directions	The ideally measurable and achievable changes and targets identified to the enterprise in response to external and internal drivers influencing the delivery and progression of the enterprise against its stated mission and vision.	From	Strategic Planning
		To	Enterprise Architecture (EA)

Information Exchange	Description		Function
Technology solution assessment	Measures of the degree of alignment and/or gap and deviation of a business and/or technology solution from the standards and/or future architecture set for the enterprise.	From	Enterprise Architecture (EA)
		To	System Development
Technology solution design	A description of the specific changes to the enterprise components that are to be implemented as a part of an investment.	From	System Development
		To	Enterprise Architecture (EA)
Technology trends	The emerging technologies and market realities, and the technical standards and technical product roadmaps and changes that are occurring external to and beyond the control of the enterprise, that are likely to present opportunities for improved strategic direction achievement, performance improvements or resource management, or place the enterprise at an increased level of risk.	From	Technology Analysis
		To	Enterprise Architecture (EA)
		To	Enterprise Architecture (EA)

Appendix – The EA Data Dictionary and Glossary

This appendix lists and describes the different types of data and documentation items referred to by the reference architecture.   As the documentation and data referred to by the reference architecture is also that used by an EA function, which is the subject of the reference architecture, then this appendix will also act as the book's glossary.

Table 31: Data Dictionary (Artefact D-8)

Data or Documentation Item	Content Category	Description	Contained Data or Documentation Item
Activities	Enterprise Component	A measurable amount of work performed to convert inputs into outputs.	
Activities with most Data Exchanges	Management View	A list of activities requiring the greatest number of information inputs and/or producing the greatest number of information outputs.	Activities
			Information Exchange
			System Data Exchange
Activity Influences	Management View	A list of the influences associated with select activities.	Activities
			Influence
Activity Model	Primitive Artefact	A functional decomposition of a functional area into the various types of activities that it's required to perform and the information that that it requires and produces in the process.	Activities
			Information Exchange
			Business Services
			Needline
Analysis	Enterprise Component	The results of analysis providing an informed assessment and/or view of the way forward.	

Data or Documentation Item	Content Category	Description	Contained Data or Documentation Item
Application	Enterprise Component	A piece of software responsible for implementing system functions and/or automating data transformations.	
Artefact	Enterprise Component	A documentation item documenting one or more EA components.	
Attributes	Enterprise Component	A discrete element of data that has been identified to help document and/or describe a thing of interest, or entity, to support the delivery of services or performance of activities.	
Business Activity Knowledge And Skill Areas	Management View	A list of the knowledge and skill areas required of persons performing the select activities.	Activities
			Knowledge and Skills
Business Architecture	Composite Artefact	A description of the structures and linkages of the services delivered, activities required to be performed and processes actually performed by the enterprise.	Activity Model
			Process Model
			Transition Plan
			Value Chain
			Business Services Model
			Business Reference Model
Business Objectives	Enterprise Component	Measurable achievements to be pursued by the business.	Performance Measures Targets
Business Performance Measures	Management View	A list of the performance measures associated with business objectives directly, or indirectly, related to select activities.	Activities
			Business Objectives
			Performance Measures
Business Plan	Composite Artefact	A high-level description of the key line of business functions and financial strategies that will accomplish the strategic goals and initiatives.	Business Objectives
			Activities Organisation Structure

Data or Documentation Item	Content Category	Description	Contained Data or Documentation Item
Business Reference Model	Primitive Artefact	The taxonomy used to describe and classify the capabilities and/or activities of the enterprise.	
Business Service Information Requirements	Management View	The information flows used and provided by select services and supporting activities.	Business Services
			Activities
			Information Exchange
Business Services	Enterprise Component	A service or product provided to a customer of the enterprise or line of business.	
Business Services Activities	Management View	The activities required to perform and support the delivery of select business services.	Business Services
			Activities
Business Services Model	Primitive Artefact	A model focusing on the key services the enterprise provides, the customers they are delivered to and the information flows associated with them.	Business Services
			Needline
			Customer
			Partner
Business service business and technology components	Management View	The activities and resources that support a business service or product.	Business Services
			EA Component
Capability	Enterprise Component	The mix of people (knowledge, experience, talent, and skill), process (activities and collaborations), and technology (application solutions and computing systems), and supporting financial and facility resources organised to deliver services.	
Change Request	Composite Artefact	A description of the changes required to component processes and resources for consideration and inclusion in the portfolio of work.	
Computer	Enterprise Component	A programmable device that performs mathematical	

Data or Documentation Item	Content Category	Description	Contained Data or Documentation Item
		calculations and logical operations, especially one that can process, store and retrieve large amounts of data very quickly.	
Concept of Operations	Composite Artefact	A description of how the business could operate to deliver a new service or existing service differently.	Future Operating Scenario
			Planning Assumption
Current Architecture	Composite Artefact	The description of the structures and linkages of all strategic, business and technology components in place and an assessment of their performance.	Strategy Architecture
			Business Architecture
			Data Architecture
			IT Systems Architecture
			Network Architecture
			Security Architecture
			Workforce Architecture
			Standards Architecture
Current Architecture Assessment	Composite Artefact	A description of the current performance and limitations of the components across all layers in support of current and target strategic directions and performance measures.	Current Architecture
			SWOT Analysis
			Performance Gap Analysis
Customer	Enterprise Component	A consumer of a business product or service of the enterprise.	
Data Architecture	Composite Artefact	A description of the structures and linkages of data and informational flows within the enterprise.	Information Exchange
			Data Model

Data or Documentation Item	Content Category	Description	Contained Data or Documentation Item
Data Model	Primitive Artefact	A model describing the structure and business rules of the data shared, used and managed by the enterprise, system or application.	Entity
Data Reference Model	Primitive Artefact	A taxonomy to be used by the enterprise to describe and classify the data shared, used and managed by the enterprise. Could be the enterprises logical data model.	Entity
EA Approach	Composite Artefact	A description of the framework, artefacts, metamodel, etc. to be used to document the EA.	EA Framework EA Method EA Artefact Standards
			Tool Usage Guidelines EA Best Practices
EA Artefact Standards	Composite Artefact	A description of what data and documentation to collect manage and/or create about enterprise strategies, processes and resources to maximise the delivery of EA services.	
EA Audit Dimension	Program Reference	An attribute that is critical to success in the measurement and management of an EA endeavour.	
EA Audit Dimension Score	Program Transaction	A rating for a given EA audit dimension.	
EA Audit Framework	Composite Artefact	A system of measuring the completeness, coverage and maturity of an EA function, used to support the ongoing tracking, reporting and management of EA.	EA Audit Dimension EA Maturity Level
EA Audit Report	Program Composite	An outlines of the current effectiveness of the EA function in terms of completeness, use and results.	EA Audit Dimension EA Audit Dimension Score

Data or Documentation Item	Content Category	Description	Contained Data or Documentation Item
EA Best Practices	Composite Artefact	A description of the proven international, national and local practices used by the organisation to plan, model and improve the enterprise.	
EA Communications Plan	Program Composite	A description of the EA program and goals. Including the EA purpose, the EA stakeholders and their roles and responsibilities, the value of EA to the enterprise and the stakeholders, the EA approach being used, the EA program schedule, and where to go to learn more about the EA program.	
EA Component	Enterprise Component	The processes and resources across all layers that contribute to the delivery of business capabilities.	
EA Component Custodians	Management View	The components and the organisational units with a custodial relationship.	Organisational Unit EA Component
EA Component Owners	Management View	A list of components and the organisational units accountable for the component.	Organisational Unit EA Component
EA Framework	Composite Artefact	A model of what the EA will document.	Segment Layer Thread
EA Management Plan	Composite Artefact	A description of the enterprise's strategic goals and initiatives, performance gaps and resource requirements, planned solutions and sequencing or transition plan, and current and future architecture summary. It should also describe the EA governance process, implementation methodology, and documentation framework.	Business Objectives Strategic Initiatives Technology Solution Designs Investments Transition Plan
EA Maturity Level	Program Reference	A classification of the different stages of development or degree	

Data or Documentation Item	Content Category	Description	Contained Data or Documentation Item
		of success achieved. To be used for the basis of scoring.	
EA Method	Composite Artefact	A method describing how EA will be performed.	
EA Question	Enterprise Component	A description of the view or analysis required of components and their linkages to support planning and oversight activities.	
Entity	Enterprise Component	A description of a real-world thing that the business needs to know about or share in order to deliver its services or do its activities.	Attributes
Future Architecture	Composite Artefact	A description of the structure and linkages of standards and components across all layers that are proposed to be addressed, used, required or implemented to meet the enterprise's vision and mission over the planning horizon.	Strategy Architecture
			Business Architecture
			Data Architecture
			IT Systems Architecture
			Network Architecture
			Security Architecture
			Workforce Architecture
			Standards Architecture
Future Information Exchanges	Management View	A list of the new and/or changed information flows within the future architecture and their deltas/gaps to the current information flows.	Information Exchange
Future Operating Scenario	Enterprise Component	A story-like narration of the way that the business could fulfil and deliver a new capability.	
			Systems Model

Data or Documentation Item	Content Category	Description	Contained Data or Documentation Item
IT Systems Architecture	Composite Artefact	A description of the structure and linkages of the components that make up a system or application.	System Function Model
			Service Reference Model
Industry EA Documentation Framework Standards	Composite Artefact	The available public and/or private EA frameworks and supporting literature.	
Influence	Enterprise Component	Something either internal or external to the control and scope of the enterprise that it needs to pay attention to, and choose to either address, leverage or ignore.	
Information Exchange	Enterprise Component	A transfer or sharing of information between roles, activities, etc.	
Balanced Scorecard	Primitive Artefact	A strategic planning and management system that is used by organisations to align business activities to the vision and strategy of the organisation, improve internal and external communications, and monitor organization performance against strategic goals.	Business Objectives
			Perspective
			Strategic Initiatives
Investment	Primitive Artefact	A description of the changes to the architecture and their rationale, dependencies, costs and timeframes.	Activities Issues Dependencies Timing Cost Rationale
Investment Activity Inter LOB Exchanges	Management View	The activities in other LOBs with which the investment activities exchange data.	Investment
			Activities
			Information Exchange
Investment Business Case	Composite Artefact	A description of the value, risk, and return on investment made in technology and other resources. Also may include alternatives analysis, program	Business Objectives
			Investment
			Technology Solution Design

Data or Documentation Item	Content Category	Description	Contained Data or Documentation Item
		performance tracking metrics, architecture information, and security status information.	
Investment Business Impact	Management View	The activities associated with and/or impacted by select investments, or strategic initiatives they implement.	Investment
			Strategic Initiatives
			Activities
Investment EA Component Impact	Management View	The component processes and resources associated with and/or impacted by select investments, or the strategic initiatives that they implement.	Investment
			Strategic Initiatives
			EA Component
Investment Overlaps	Management View	A list of the components associated with two or more investments, to help identify overlaps.	Change Request
			Investment
			EA Component
Investment Performance Measure Status	Management View	A list of the performance metrics applicable to select investments, and an assessment of their progress against the targets.	Investment
			Performance Measures
			Targets
Investment to Strategic Initiative	Management View	A list of the investments and strategic initiatives that they implement.	Investment
			Strategic Initiatives
Investment with no Strategic Initiatives	Management View	A list of the Investments that are not linked to any Strategic Initiatives.	Investment
			Strategic Initiatives
Issues	Enterprise Component	Known problems associated with the investment requiring attention.	
Knowledge Management Plan	Composite Artefact	A description of how knowledge, information, and data are shared across the enterprise, including descriptions and diagrams of information sharing between systems, applications, knowledge warehouses, and databases. Also commonly referred to as an Information Management Plan.	

Data or Documentation Item	Content Category	Description	Contained Data or Documentation Item
Knowledge and Skills	Enterprise Component	A description of the information and concepts required to be understood, and the experience and activities to be performed, by a role within an enterprise.	
Layer	Composite Artefact	A sub-architecture of EA responsible for the description of the structure and linkages of a related set of components.	
Line of business services	Management View	A list of the services delivered or proposed for delivery by select lines of business.	Business Services
Logical Data Model	Primitive Artefact	A model describing the entities, or real word objects, and their relationships the need to be managed or understood to effectively deliver a service or undertake an activity.	Entities
			Relationships
EA Modelling Guidelines	Composite Artefact	The standards, recommendations and suggestions on how to describe, document and represent EA components to best support the attainment of EA objectives and the delivery of EA services.	
Needline	Enterprise Component	The direction of information flow between different operational or system areas.	
Needline information flows	Management View	The information flows associated with the needlines between select operational or system nodes.	Needline
			Information Exchange
Network Architecture	Composite Artefact	The description of the structure and linkages of network components within the enterprise, including transmission equipment, software and communication protocols, and infrastructure (wired and wireless), that support transmission of data and	Networks Model

Data or Documentation Item	Content Category	Description	Contained Data or Documentation Item
		connectivity between other EA components.	
Network Components	Enterprise Component	The components implementing the technologies delivering the enterprise's voice, data and video network.	
Networks Model	Primitive Artefact	A description of the physical connections between the enterprise's voice, data, and video network components, including external Wide Area Networks (WANs) and Local Area Networks (LANs), also called 'extranets' and 'intranets'.	Computer
			Network Components
Operational Node	Enterprise Component	A physical or figurative location within the enterprise where activities are performed. For example, a geographic location or organisational unit.	
Organisation Activities	Management View	The activities performed by select organisational unit(s).	Organisational Unit
			Activities
Organisation Structure	Primitive Artefact	A description of the structure and linkages of organisational units.	Organisational Unit
Organisational Unit	Enterprise Component	A business unit, division, team or position within the organisation.	
Partner	Enterprise Component	An external party to the enterprise that provides products or services to the enterprise.	
Performance Gap Analysis	Primitive Artefact	A summary of the performance, functional and technical gaps in the current architecture against previous target performance measures.	Performance Measures
Performance Measure Status	Program Transaction	An assessment of the current value or rating of a performance measure against its planned or target value or rating.	

Data or Documentation Item	Content Category	Description	Contained Data or Documentation Item
Performance Measures	Program Reference	The thing to be measured to determine whether a business objective has been achieved.	
Perspective	Enterprise Component	The classifications of business objectives identifying the stakeholder group with the greatest vested interest in its achievement.	
Physical Data Model	Primitive Artefact	A description of the physical data objects and their relationships as they have been programmed into a database management system or other type of data store.	
Planning Assumption	Enterprise Component	The changes to the current architecture processes, technology and people required to meet the scenario outlined.	
Priority Activitles	Management View	The activities deemed strategically important, or with priority business performance issues.	Activities
			Influence or
			Business Objectives
Priority Information Exchanges with no System Data Exchange	Management View	The priority information flows that are not supported by automation.	Information Exchange System Data Exchange
Process Model	Primitive Artefact	A model that describes the sequence of steps undertaken to complete the delivery of a service, or of the actions to be taken in response to some trigger.	Activities
Project Overview	Enterprise Component	A description of the scope, intent and status of the changes associated with an approved, scheduled or in-progress project.	Business Objectives
			Investment Business Case
			Technology Solution Design
Project Portfolio			Project Overview

Data or Documentation Item	Content Category	Description	Contained Data or Documentation Item
	Primitive Artefact	A list of planned, and in progress, changes to the enterprise.	Investment
Reference Model	Primitive Artefact	A taxonomy of items used to classify components and to illustrate the breadth and depth of potential alternatives.	Business Reference Model
			Data Reference Model
			Service Reference Model
			Technical Reference Model
SWOT Analysis	Primitive Artefact	An assessment of various internal and external influences and the positive and/or negative impacts that they may have on the enterprise.	Influence
Security Architecture	Composite Artefact	A detailed description of all aspects of the system that relate to security, along with a set of principles to guide the design.	Security Plan
Security Plan	Composite Artefact	A description of the security programs that are in effect throughout the enterprise to mitigate the risks to the operations and credibility of the enterprise.	
Segment	Enterprise Component	A vertical or horizontal functional area of the business for which EA is to be performed.	
Service Components	Enterprise Component	A process or resource that delivers predetermined functionality exposed through or defined by a business or technical interface.	
Service Components to System Functions	Management View	The systems functions that realize and/or support business and enterprise services.	Service Components
			Systems Functions
Service Reference Model	Primitive Artefact	The taxonomy of Business and Enterprise Services to be used by the enterprise to describe the	

Data or Documentation Item	Content Category	Description	Contained Data or Documentation Item
		candidate and implemented cross-LOB or horizontal services within the enterprise.	
Standards Architecture	Composite Artefact	A description of the structure and linkages of the products, specifications and best practices used by an enterprise.	Technical Service Standards Forecast
			Technical Service Standards Profile
Standards and asset management data	Composite Artefact	Existing information about standards and asset plans maintained separately from the enterprise architecture.	
Strategic Capability Assessment	Composite Artefact	The capabilities of the enterprise, those that a merger or acquisition target has, and the strategic initiatives associated with the capabilities.	Capability
			Strategic Initiatives
Strategic Initiatives	Enterprise Component	The enabling programs and projects identified to help achieve the objectives an enterprise has set for itself.	
Strategic Initiatives without Capabilities	Management View	A list of the strategic initiatives and the current capabilities to support their implementation or delivery.	Strategic Initiatives
			Capability
Strategic Plan	Composite Artefact	A high-level policy and planning document that an enterprise uses to document its direction, competitive strategy, most important goals, and the enabling programs and projects (strategic initiatives).	Business Objectives
			Strategic Initiatives
Strategy Architecture	Composite Artefact	A description of the structure and linkages of the influences, goals and initiatives of an enterprise.	Strategic Plan
			SWOT Analysis
			Balanced Scorecard
Strategy Map	Composite Artefact	A diagrammatic representation of how the organisation plans to achieve its mission and vision by means of a linked chain of continuous improvements from	Business Objectives

Data or Documentation Item	Content Category	Description	Contained Data or Documentation Item
		a financial, customer, internal process and learning and growth perspective.	
System Node	Enterprise Component	A physical or figurative location within the enterprise where system functions are deployed or accessed. For example, a physical device or desktop.	
Strategy to Business Activities	Management View	The relationships between strategy components and business activities.	Business Objectives
			Strategic Initiatives
			Activities
Strategy to EA Components	Management View	The relationships between strategy components and business and technology process and resource components.	Business Objectives
			Strategic Initiatives
			EA Component
System Data Exchange	Enterprise Component	The data flows provided and consumed by Systems and Applications.	
System Function Gaps	Management View	A list of required system functions versus those provided by select applications.	Systems Functions
			Investment
			Application
System Function Model	Primitive Artefact	A model describing the automated data transformations and exchanges performed within or by an application or system.	Systems Functions
System Functions to Applications	Management View	The system functions implemented by one of more systems or applications.	Systems Functions
			Application
Systems Functions	Enterprise Component	The data process logic, transformations, presentations, etc. performed or automated by system or application.	
Systems Model	Primitive Artefact	Documentation of the Systems that perform System Functions.	Application
Targets	Enterprise Component	The dates, values and units to be achieved.	

Data or Documentation Item	Content Category	Description	Contained Data or Documentation Item
Technical Reference Model	Primitive Artefact	The taxonomy of Technical Services to be used by the enterprise to describe and classify the various types of candidate and implemented hardware, software, technical specifications and standards across the enterprise.	Technical Services
Technical Service Standards Forecast	Primitive Artefact	The short, medium and long-term forecasts for a Technical Service and the Technologies themselves.	Technical Reference Model
Technical Service Standards Profile	Primitive Artefact	A list of the international, national and local standards (protocols, frameworks, best practices and products) associated with each Technical Service.	Technology Technical Reference Model
Technology	Enterprise Component	The product, protocol or specification that fulfils a particular Technical Service.	
Technology Component	Enterprise Component	An implementation of a Technology	
Technology Component KSAs	Management View	The KSAs associated with select Technology Components	Technology Knowledge and Skills
Technology Reference Model Components	Management View	The Service Components and Technical Services and their implementing EA components.	EA Component Service Reference Model Technical Reference Model Data Reference Model
Technology Solution Alignment Assessment	Composite Artefact	An assessment of a proposed technology solution design against the standards and future architecture for compliance and fit.	

Data or Documentation Item	Content Category	Description	Contained Data or Documentation Item
Technology Solution Design	Composite Artefact	A description of the enterprise component changes in terms of standards, products, vendors, etc. proposed for implementation to enable the delivery of the outputs and/or outcomes of a project.	Systems Functions
			System Data Exchange
			Application
			Technology
			Computer
			Network Components
Technology Standards Gaps	Management View	The technology standards profile mapped to the applications for fit and compliance.	
Thread	Enterprise Component	A sub-architecture of the EA that relates to each layer of the EA.	
Timing	Enterprise Component	Commencement Date and Duration of an activity.	
Tool Usage Guidelines	Composite Artefact	Outlines the current policies and procedures associated with the access and use of the EA tool for supporting documentation, etc.	
Transition Plan	Composite Artefact	List of investments (projects) and their timeframes and dependencies.	Investment
Value Chain	Primitive Artefact	A high-level logical ordering of business processes that provides an overview of how value (i.e. product or service) is produced.	Activities
Workforce Architecture	Composite Artefact	A description of the organisational structure and the linkages to the people, roles and responsibilities within the enterprise.	Organisation Structure
			Workforce Plan
			Knowledge and Skills
Workforce Plan	Composite Artefact	A high-level policy and planning document to describe how the enterprise intends to align its needs and priorities with those of its workforce to ensure it can meet its legislative, regulatory,	

Data or Documentation Item	Content Category	Description	Contained Data or Documentation Item
		service and production requirements and objectives.	

Appendix – EA Function Key Technical Service Requirements

In Section 5 – The Networks and Infrastructure of the EA function, in response to the question, What technical services are the EA function's technology solutions likely to require?, an indicative list of Technical Services where highlighted. In this appendix the descriptions of these technical services, sourced from the US Federal EA (FEA, OMB) Technology Reference Model, are provided to help explain what they are and why they may be required.

Table 32: EA Function Key Technical Service Requirements (Management View)

Service Area	Service Category	Service Standard	Description
Component Framework	Data Interchange	Data Exchange	Data Exchange is concerned with the sending of data over a communications network and the definition of data communicated from one application to another. Data Exchange provides the communications common denominator between disparate systems.
	Data Management	Database Connectivity	Defines the protocol or method in which an application connects to a data store or data base.
		Reporting and Analysis	Consist of the tools, languages and protocols used to extract data from a data store and process it into useful information.
	User Presentation / Interface	Content Rendering	This defines the software and protocols used for transforming data for presentation in a graphical user interface.

Service Area	Service Category	Service Standard	Description
		Dynamic / Server-Side Display	This consists of the software that is used to create graphical user interfaces with the ability to change while the program is running.
		Static Display	Static Display consists of the software protocols that are used to create a predefined, unchanging graphical interface between the user and the software.
Service Access and Delivery	Access Channels	Collaboration / Communications	Define the forms of electronic exchange of messages, documents or other information. Electronic communication provides efficiency through expedited time of delivery.
		Web Browser	Define the program that serves as your front end to the World Wide Web on the Internet. In order to view a site, you type its address (URL) into the browser's location field.
	Delivery Channels	Extranet	An Extranet is a private network that uses the Internet protocol and the public telecommunication system to securely share part of a business's information or operations with suppliers, vendors, partners, customers or other businesses. An extranet can be viewed as part of a company's intranet that is extended to users outside the company.
		Intranet	An Intranet is a private network that is contained within an enterprise. It may consist of many interlinked local area networks and is used to share company information and resources among employees.
	Service Requirements	Authentication / Single Sign-on (SSO)	Refers to a method that provides users with the ability to login one time only, and getting authenticated access to all their applications and resources.

Service Area	Service Category	Service Standard	Description
Service Interface and Integration	Interoperability	Data Transformation	Data Transformation consists of the protocols and languages that change the presentation of data within a graphical user interface or application.
		Data Types / Validation	Refers to specifications used in identifying and affirming common structures and processing rules. This technique is referenced and abstracted from the content document or source data.
Service Platform and Infrastructure	Database / Storage	Database	Refers to a collection of information organised in such a way that a computer program can quickly select desired pieces of data. A database management system (DBMS) is a software application providing management, administration, performance, and analysis tools for databases.
	Delivery Servers	Application Servers	In a three-tier environment, a separate computer (application server) performs the business logic, although some part may still be handled by the user's machine. After the Web exploded in the mid 1990s, application servers became Web based.
	Hardware / Infrastructure	Servers / Computers	This refers to the various types of programmable machines which are capable of responding to sets of instructions and executing programs.
	Software Engineering	Modelling	Technology that supports the process of representing entities, data, business logic, and capabilities for aiding in software engineering.

Appendix – The Standards Thread for the Reference Architecture

In Section 6 – The Standards Thread of the EA function, the specific standards required for the EA function were discussed. It outlined the key standards areas of differentiation for the EA function and that the reference architecture and EA^3 can be used as the based standards in these areas. This appendix in turn outlines the standards in each of these areas for the reference architecture. In the main, they represent the example/recommended elements outlined within EA^3.

The EA Framework

The EA^3 framework and concepts formed the basis of the reference architecture. These are summarised in the Introduction section and expanded on and documented throughout the reference architecture.

The EA Methodology

As the development of the reference architecture is not in itself the execution of an EA function, the EA^3 method was not strictly followed.

The EA Best Practices

As with the EA Framework element, the EA^3 list of best practices was used as the baseline for the derivation, modelling and documentation of the reference architecture. Listed below are brief introductions to each of the key practices used or followed during its development:

- SWOT Analysis, to help consolidate the various drivers and influences on Enterprise Architecture.
- Kaplan and Norton's Balanced Scorecard approach to determine and document the strategic intent and requirements of the broader enterprise, and the outputs and enablers of the EA function.

- The Department of Defense Architecture Framework (DoDAF) Activity-based Method (ABM) operational views and IDEF0 to rigorously define the business functions and information flow requirements of the EA function.
- Class modelling for annotating the conceptual and logical metamodel of the EA function and repository solution.
- The DoDAF ABM system views to rigorously define the system functionality and architecture models.
- The Federal Enterprise Architecture (FEA) Service Reference Model (SRM), to define the list of business and enterprise services that an EA function may need, and look to reuse.
- The Federal Enterprise Architecture (FEA) Technical Reference Model (TRM), to highlight the key technical services that are likely to be required or used to support the implementation of it systems

The EA Artefacts

The EA[3] list of example and recommended artefacts is a complete set of data and documentation covering all layers and threads of an architecture across various levels of abstraction.

As the purpose and intent, and breadth and depth of the reference architecture is different from an actual EA, some of the artefacts are either not relevant, or only partially relevant. In Table 33 is the complete list of example/recommended EA[3] artefacts and an indicator and/or brief explanation of whether it was used, and how and why.

Table 33: EA[3] Artefact List

EA[3] Cube Level	#	Artefact Name (*Composite Artefact)	Used and How (if applicable)
Strategic Goals & Initiatives (S)	S-1	Strategic Plan	No
	S-2	SWOT Analysis	Yes
	S-3	Concept of Operations Scenario	Yes
	S-4	Concept of Operations Diagram	Yes
	S-5	Balanced Scorecard™	Yes
Business Products & Services (B)	B-1	Business Plan*	No. Though the reference architecture provides much content similar or input to a business plan
	B-2	Node Connectivity Diagram	Yes

EA³ Cube Level	#	Artefact Name (*Composite Artefact)	Used and How (if applicable)
	B-3	Swim Lane Process Diagram *	Partially. As sequence diagrams to highlight the key exchanges of data with the EA function
	B-4	Business Process/Service Model	Yes
	B-5	Business Process/Product Matrix *	Partially. The EA Program and Transition Plan discusses various service scenarios the EA function may fulfil
	B-6	Use Case Narrative & Diagram	Yes
	B-7	Investment Business Case *	Partially. The EA Program and Transition Plan discusses various service scenarios the EA function may fulfil
Data & Information (D)	D-1	Knowledge Management Plan	Partially - A description of the type of IT functionality appropriate to the type of information gathered and shared is provided
	D-2	Information Exchange Matrix *	Yes
	D-3	Object State-Transition Diagram	No. Determined too low level a detail for the purpose of the book
	D-4	Object Event Sequence Diagram	Yes
	D-5	Logical Data Model	Yes
	D-6	Physical Data Model	Yes. The IBM Rational System Architect metamodel
	D-7	Activity/Entity (CRUD) Matrix *	Yes
	D-8	Data Dictionary/Object Library	Yes
Systems & Applications (SA)	SA-1	System Interface Diagram	Yes
	SA-2	System Communication Description	No
	SA-3	System Interface Matrix *	No
	SA-4	System Data Flow Diagram	Partially. The system function decomposition of the EA

EA³ Cube Level	#	Artefact Name (*Composite Artefact)	Used and How (if applicable)
			Management System is provided
	SA-5	System/Operations Matrix *	Yes
	SA-6	Systems Data Exchange Matrix *	No
	SA-7	System Performance Matrix *	No
	SA-8	System Evolution Diagram	No
	SA-9	Web Application Diagram	No
Networks and Infrastructure (NI)	NI-1	Network Connectivity Diagram	No
	NI-2	Network Inventory	No
	NI-3	Capital Equipment Inventory	No
	NI-4	Building Blueprints *	No
	NI-5	Network Centre Diagram	No
	NI-6	Cable Plant Diagram	No
	NI-7	Rack Elevation Diagram	No

The EA Tool and Repository

To aid the modelling, documentation, analysis and reporting on the reference architecture, IBM Rational's System Architect (SA) was used. SA is one of the leading software applications targeting the delivery of EA Management services, providing a number of functions and features to support the management of the type of data and information specifically associated with EA. For example, the following SA system functions and features were used:

- DoDAF ABM framework – for providing many of the base models, linkages and automations
- Report Generator - for generating the tables within the reference architecture
- Batch Document Facility - for the automatic refresh of the tables
- Heat Map Manager - for highlighting impacted enterprise components on the figures
- Matrix utility - for the capture and reporting of key linkages
- SA Rest Service - for the automation of diagram refreshes
- Metamodel extensions – to enable the capture and analysis of additional data and linkages specifically required as part of the reference architecture not available by default.

- Custom macros – to automate the population of certain objects and figures.

Illustrated as a UML class diagram, in Figure 42 is a logical view of the components documented and links maintained within System Architect to support the reference architecture is provided. A combination of standard 'out of the box' objects and links, and custom objects and links, was used to support the reporting and analysis presented throughout the book.

Figure 42: Logical SA Metamodel (Artefact D-5)

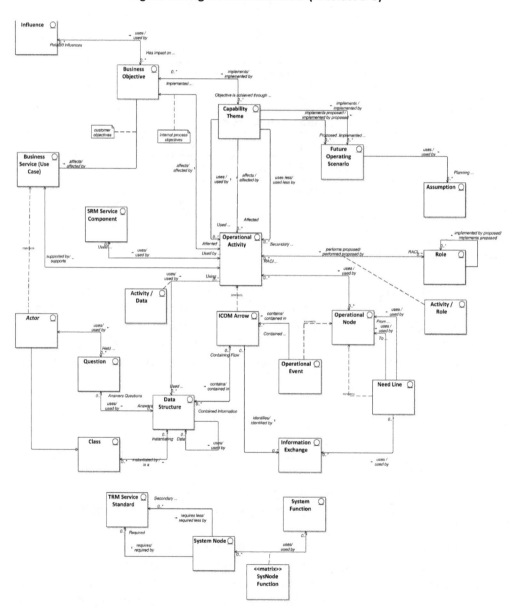

Appendix – EA Function Horse Blanket

Figure 43: EA Function Horse Blanket (Management View)

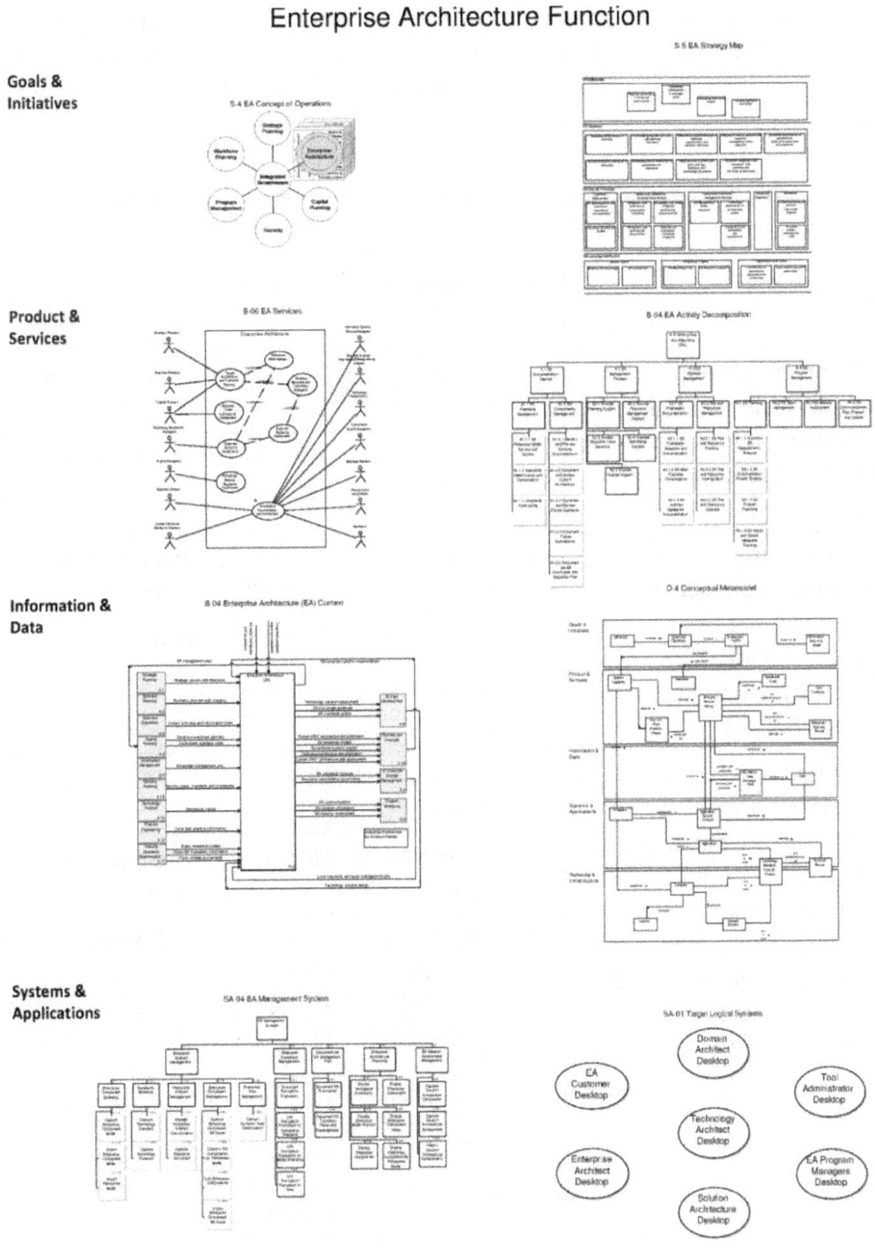

Enterprise Architecture Function

Appendix – EA Storyboard Details

This appendix lists the text on each of the storyboards in the section 'What are the key business and technology components to be established or enhanced?' and the EA components at each layer of the architecture that are key or the primary focus of the storyboard.

Table 34: Strategic Alignment and Cross-LOB Priority Components

Priority Overview	#	Component Type	Name
Improving planning of IT investments from strategic goals and initiatives and resource planning from across the enterprise.		Business Objective	Increased enterprise-wide and LOB planning decisions
		Business Objective	Improving effectiveness of planning
Help the enterprise to identify, assess and review business and technology drivers and needs for change, and identify, describe and communicate the associated changes.		Use Case	Target Architecture and Transition Planning
		Use Case	Enterprise-Wide Analysis
		Use Case	Strategy, Business and Technology Evaluation
For an agreed area/segment, identify, document and assess the current architecture, work with process and resource owners to define the future architecture and document the plan. Work with planners and delivery personnel to understand the plan.	1.2	Operational Activity	EA Components Management
	1.2.1	Operational Activity	Identify and Review Existing Documentation
	1.2.2	Operational Activity	Document and Assess Current Architecture
	1.2.3	Operational Activity	Document and Review Future Scenarios
	1.2.4	Operational Activity	Document Future Architecture
	1.2.5	Operational Activity	Document the EA Summaries and Sequence Plan

Priority Overview	#	Component Type	Name
Information will be sourced from various planning and operational functions to get a view of the current strategic, business and technology drivers. The principal information provided will be in the form of the integrated current and future architectures and EA management plan.		ICOM Arrow	Strategic drivers and directions
		ICOM Arrow	Business priorities and changes
		ICOM Arrow	Knowledge management plan
		ICOM Arrow	Technology trends
		ICOM Arrow	Investment business case
		ICOM Arrow	Current activities and information flows
		ICOM Arrow	Existing investment portfolio
		ICOM Arrow	Security plans, standards and procedures
		ICOM Arrow	Current SBT architecture and assessment
		ICOM Arrow	Future SBnT architecture documentation
All components across all layers of the EA framework need to be taken into consideration to a level appropriate to the constraints on the strategic or cross-line of business architecture being performed.			
Automate the capture, interpretation, gap and overlap analysis of the various types of data with a view to compiling the EA management plan.	1.1.1	System Function	Enterprise Component Modelling
	1.1.2	System Function	Standards Modelling
	1.1.3	System Function	Composite Artefact Management
	1.1.4	System Function	Enterprise Component Management
	1.1.5	System Function	Enterprise View Management
	1.3	System Function	Document the EA Management Plan

Priority Overview	#	Component Type	Name
Enable Enterprise Architects to efficiently capture, analyse and manage the portfolios of required components and component adjustments to facilitate production of the EA management plan.		System Node	Enterprise Architect Desktop

Table 35: Redundancy Assessment and Standards Enforcement Priority Components (Management View)

Priority Overview	#	Component Type	Name
Focus on ensuring consistency of implementation and reducing the complexity and duplication of components across the enterprise.		Business Objective	Increased integration from enterprise-wide planning and utilisation of resources
		Business Objective	Standardisation of information on processes and resources
Help resource management by improving visibility of costly and/or poorly-performing duplicate business and technology processes and resources.		Use Case	Technology Solution Alignment Assessment
		Use Case	Duplicate Resource Assessment
		Use Case	Duplicate Resource Identification
		Use Case	Business Case Architectural Assessment
Assess the current state, classify resources, and help define, document and share agreed standards.	1.1.1	Operational Activity	EA Reference Model Review and Update
	1.1.2	Operational Activity	Standards Identification and Consolidation
	1.1.3	Operational Activity	Standards Forecasting
	1.2.1	Operational Activity	Identify and Review Existing Documentation
	1.2.2	Operational Activity	Document and Assess Current Architecture
		ICOM Arrow	EA standards forecast

Priority Overview	#	Component Type	Name
Information will be principally sourced from current business operations and provided in the form of standards forecasts and resource consolidation opportunities.		ICOM Arrow	Resource consolidation opportunities
		ICOM Arrow	Current activities and information flows
Assess and document the business and/or technology processes and/or resource components relevant to the business, enterprise or technical services under investigation.		Class	Technology Standard/Protocol/Product
		Class	Business Reference Model
		Class	Service Reference Model
		Class	Technical Reference Model
In addition to the typical enterprise artefact management, to capture the results of assessment activities and define standards profiles and forecasts. Facilitating decision-making on these, and solution assessment against these, will greatly improve integration, compliance and compliance measurement and management.	1.1	System Function	Enterprise Artefact Management
	1.4	System Function	Enterprise Architecture Reporting
	1.5	System Function	EA Solution Assessment Management
Facilitate access to those responsible for identifying opportunities for reuse and preferred implementations so that they can easily identify and confidently design compliant solutions.		System Node	Domain Architect Desktop
		System Node	Technology Architect Desktop
		System Node	EA Customer Desktop
		System Node	Solution Architecture Desktop

Table 36: Documentation and Assessment Priority Components

Priority Overview	#	Component Type	Name
Facilitate communications across governance function activities and reduce		Business Objective	Increased visualisation of valuable and duplicative processes and resources

Priority Overview	#	Component Type	Name
misinterpretation of requirements, processes and resources.		Business Objective	Reduced misunderstandings of resource requirements and potential solutions
Provide information about architectural components specifically of relevance to the other governance functions in a usable and accessible form.		Use Case	Architecture Documentation and Assessment
Build a view of the current state of the enterprise's architecture for use and access by EA customers.	1.1.1	Operational Activity	EA Reference Model Review and Update
	1.1.2	Operational Activity	Standards Identification and Consolidation
	1.2.1	Operational Activity	Identify and Review Existing Documentation
	1.2.2	Operational Activity	Document and Assess Current Architecture
Documentation and assessment for the current state will come from both planning and operations sources. The results will be views into the architecture and assessment of current standards, processes and resources, and plans appropriate to the requirements of the EA customer.		ICOM Arrow	Strategic drivers and directions
		ICOM Arrow	Business priorities and changes
		ICOM Arrow	Knowledge management plan
		ICOM Arrow	Technology trends
		ICOM Arrow	Investment business case
		ICOM Arrow	Current activities and information flows
		ICOM Arrow	Existing investment portfolio
		ICOM Arrow	Security plans, standards and procedures
		ICOM Arrow	Strategic drivers and directions
		ICOM Arrow	Business priorities and changes
		ICOM Arrow	Knowledge management plan
		ICOM Arrow	Technology trends
		ICOM Arrow	Investment business case
		ICOM Arrow	Current activities and information flows
		ICOM Arrow	Existing investment portfolio

Priority Overview	#	Component Type	Name
		ICOM Arrow	Security plans, standards and procedures
Any core component types from across the layers may be the subject of the documentation and analysis, depending on the requirements of the EA customer.			
Critical to success of documentation and assessment on behalf of EA customers will be the publication of the results in a way that will allow the EA customer to action, consume and use the information.	1.1	System Function	Enterprise Artefact Management
	1.3	System Function	Document the EA Management Plan
Deliver the reporting functionality to the component documentation and assessments directly to EA customer desktops.		System Node	Enterprise Architect Desktop
		System Node	EA Customer Desktop

Appendix – Bibliography and Additional Suggested Reading

ADV, EATP	Course material from Dr Bernard's EA Training Program, Advanced EA.
AGA, V3	*Australian Government Architecture Reference Models* Australian Government Information Management Office agimo.gov.au/policy-guides-procurement/australian-government-architecture-aga/aga-rm/
AIEA, 2005	*An Introduction to Enterprise Architecture, 2nd Edition* by Scott A. Bernard, PhD Authorhouse 2005
CSFEAE, 2007	*Critical Success Factors for EA Effectiveness.* by L. DeBoever EADirections [EA-7003]. http://www.eadirections.com/uploads/Critical_Success_Factors.pdf
EAAF, OMB	*EA Assessment Framework (EAAF)* The U.S. Office of Management and Budget www.whitehouse.gov/omb/e-gov/eaaf
EAaS, 2006	*Enterprise Architecture as Strategy* by Jeanne W. Ross, Peter Weill and David C. Robertson Harvard Business School Press 2006
EAMMF, GAO	*A Framework for Assessing and Improving EA Management (Version 2.0)* U.S. Government Accountability Office www.gao.gov/products/GAO-10-846G
EAP, 1992	*Enterprise Architecture Planning, Developing a Blueprint for Data, Applications and Technology* by Steve H. Spewak with Steven C. Hill. Wiley & Sons. 1992
FEA, OMB	*Federal Enterprise Architecture* The U.S. Office of Management and Budget

	www.whitehouse.gov/omb/e-gov/fea/
FSAM, OMB	Federal Segment Architecture Methodology, Version 1.0 The U.S. Office of Management and Budget www.whitehouse.gov/omb/e-gov/fsam
FUN, EATP	Course material from Dr Bernard's EA Training Program, Fundamentals of EA
NAVSO, P-5239-04	Information Systems Security Manager (ISSM) Guidebook, Module 04, Information Systems Security (Infosec), Program Guidelines
NFAEAAP, 2009	*A Need for Formalization and Auditing in Enterprise Architecture Approaches and Programs* by Scott Bernard and John Grasso Journal of Enterprise Architecture, May 2009
WIKIPEDIA	Accessed online during manuscript development
WITBGEA, CC, 7, 8	*What It Takes to Be a Great Enterprise Architect* by Dana Bredemeyer and Ruth Malan Cutter Consortium, Executive Report, Vol. 7, No. 8

About the Author

Phil Woodworth has over twenty-five years' experience in information technology (IT). Phil has consulted and contracted to numerous organisations in all stages of IT change management and implementation, including IT strategy development and planning; enterprise architecture and enterprise-wide solution architecture; systems and application design and development; and testing and training.

Phil has developed enterprise architectures and helped establish, enable and mentor enterprise architecture practices for several public and private sector organisations. He is also an instructor of Dr. Scott Bernard's enterprise architecture training program. His current areas of research, teaching and consulting include optimisation of business and IT alignment and governance, IT initiative identification, planning and oversight, and enterprise architecture.

Index

CPSIA information can be obtained
at www.ICGtesting.com
Printed in the USA
FSHW012028240719
60377FS